SILENT
ISSUES
OF THE
CHURCH

CARL H. LUNDQUIST

SILENT ISSUES OF THE CHURCH

Though intended for personal reading and profit, this book is part of the Victor Adult Elective Series and therefore is also intended for group study. A Leader's Guide with Victor Multiuse Transparency Masters is available from your local bookstore.

VICTOR

BOOKS a division of SP Publications, Inc.
WHEATON, ILLINOIS 60187

Offices also in
Whitby, Ontario, Canada
Amersham-on-the-Hill, Bucks, England

Unless otherwise noted, Bible quotations are from *The Holy Bible: New International Version*, © 1973, 1978, 1984 by the New York International Bible Society and used by permission of Zondervan Bible Publishers. Other quotations are from the *American Standard Version* (ASV); *The New Testament in Modern English* (PH), © J.B. Phillips, by permission of Macmillan Publishing Co. and Collins Publishers; and the *King James Version* (KJV).

Recommended Dewey Decimal Classification: 241.3

Suggested Subject Headings: BEHAVIOR: CHRISTIAN LIFE: SIN: CONSCIENCE

Library of Congress Catalog Card Number: 85-50309

ISBN: 0-89693-721-6

Revised edition © 1985 by SP Publications, Inc.
First edition © 1984 by Harvest Publications.

CONTENTS

Introduction

*In loving
dedication
to Nancy,
my wife
and
soul friend
in a
lifetime
of joyous
discipleship
under Christ
our Lord.*

INTRODUCTION

For twenty-eight years as president of Bethel College and Seminary in St. Paul, Minnesota, I enjoyed the privilege of working with thousands of inspiring and committed Christian students. I concluded my tenure in 1982 more optimistic than ever about the church's future because of the spiritual qualities I saw in young people—tomorrow's leaders.

Over the years I have discussed the themes of this book with students, as well as thoughtful faculty colleagues and pastors. Not everyone has agreed with me, but everyone has recognized the need for ongoing dialogue on campus and in the church.

The problems discussed here tend to be *silent* issues of the church. Many pastors hesitate to deal with them from the pulpit, and understandably so. Not all issues are clearly black and white. The Bible in its timelessness does not always deal with the problems of a specific age or culture. And its broad principles have been interpreted differently by equally devout people.

Consequently, most pastors generally say nothing about these issues. And as a result, a whole new generation is growing up hearing little from the pulpit about temptations in personal living. The youth are left to form their own value systems under peer pressure more than under biblical teaching.

A few pastors also have placed such an emphasis on positive

preaching that they shrink from calling on their people to say *no* in behavioral matters.

Church leaders and individual Christians seem equally silent on these issues. Perhaps taking the lead from these pastors, they join in stressing the positive rather than challenging people to say no to practices which can lead to serious spiritual problems.

I acknowledge that the issues discussed in this book are not the major ones confronting the church today in its power struggle with the forces of evil in the world. But others are addressing those issues.

My purpose is to sound an alert about the erosion of evangelical standards of personal lifestyle so that in a spirit of self-discipline we will dare to say *no* to our culture and to practices that I believe are out of harmony with God's Word. In doing so, we will be walking in the noblest traditions of the Christian church.

ONE

A TIME TO SAY NO

Well-known radio and television preacher Charles Swindoll tells of an experiment in a high-school science class in which students placed a frog in a large beaker on a low-flame Bunsen burner. As the flame heated the beaker, the temperature rose so slowly that the frog never noticed a change. In time, it was dead, without ever attempting to jump to safety.

Concludes Swindoll: "Deterioration is never sudden. No garden suddenly overgrows with thorns. No church suddenly splits. No building suddenly crumbles. No marriage suddenly breaks down. No nation suddenly becomes mediocre. Slowly, almost imperceptibly, certain things are accepted that once were rejected. Things once considered hurtful are now tolerated. The gap grows wider as moral erosion joins hands with spiritual decay."[1]

MANY WON'T SAY NO

Like the unsuspecting frog, countless Christians today are unaware of the dangers that have grown out of the culture surrounding them. Slowly, they are being lulled into complacency, unconcerned that their spiritual lives are slowly deteriorating. At the root of the problem is undisciplined behavior—a refusal to say *no* to personal temptations. To say no seems too harsh, negative, judgmental, confrontational, final. To many evangelical believers, the word *no* in our Western world of affluence and indulgence doesn't sound right. Consequently, no is seldom heard at home, school, work, or even church.

Annually, an estimated 400,000 babies are born in America to unmarried girls and women. In addition, in 1984 nearly a million unmarried women in the United States had abortions. All of this represents tragic evidence of the growing inability to say no. The current abortionist argument that a woman should have control over her body could be advanced earlier in the reproductive process. Instead of saying no to the birth of her baby, the unmarried woman in control of her body would be smarter to say no the initial immorality. But because prebirth infanticide has been legalized, the call to moral self-discipline has been weakened.

Unmarried mothers, of course, are not the only people who engage in casual sex. Sex researchers estimate that 30 to 50 percent of all married partners can't say no to adultery. Among them are certain congressmen who couldn't say no, and their amorous adventures made titillating headlines. Many corporate women officers newly arrived in the executive suite also can't say no, and a new set of management problems has developed as a result. Church congregations have split because of pastors who have forsaken their high calling for illicit love. As the president of a theological seminary, I always was grieved and sometimes felt betrayed by graduates who succumbed at this point. It was a major blow to me to learn of two evangelical pastors who from their pulpits emphasized the deeper Christian life but engaged in clandestine affairs with their secretaries.

The word *no* also is not heard in many other areas of life. Otherwise, with all we know about lung cancer and emphysema, why are 20 percent of men and even more women still smoking cigarettes? (Happily, the percentage went down slightly this past year but not enough.)

Ten million alcoholics in the U.S. may wish they had said no to their first drink. And millions addicted to drugs would be free from their bondage if they had said no the first time. Then there are the gamblers who couldn't say no to bets on horses, dogs, cards, or sporting events to the tune of an estimated $50 billion a year. And what about those of us lugging those extra pounds? Although we know a great deal about calories and cholesterol, many of us can't say no to excessive food or to indolent living.

At the highest levels of government, even when the administration identifies publicly with traditional moral values, key people have not always said no to questionable ethical practices. As a result, in recent years several officials have been forced to resign from their federal positions and some have gone to prison.

The inability to say *no* to temptation has left the whole moral landscape clouded. Estimates indicate that banks lose more money from unpublicized embezzlement by their employees than from robberies. A *New York Times* survey on cheating in high school quotes one student as saying, "Most people who cheat don't feel they're doing anything wrong." Another student viewed cheating positively, saying, "A person cheats because he wants to do better on a test. Some people don't care enough to cheat."

Fraudulent long-distance telephone calls in a recent year cost AT&T $108 million, a charge borne ultimately by its customers through higher rates. Some of America's largest corporations recently have been fined for briberies, falsifying invoices, or avoiding customs fees to have a better bottom line. Americans currently commit upward of 12 million felonies annually. Federal and state prisons are bulging with nearly half a million inmates and at the present rate an incredible five million could be in correctional custody by 1990.

Half of all Americans are afraid of being robbed or mugged when they walk streets in their neighborhoods. Assaults on public school teachers by students appear underreported at 130,000 a year. From 1960 to 1973 the homicide rate in the U.S. doubled and now is 9 times that of England or Japan. Simultaneously, capital punishment has been viewed with increasing approval so that today 72 percent of the population favor it. Scofflaws abound—speeders, shoplifters, graffiti scribblers, jaywalkers, hazardous waste dumpers, arsonists.

Says Dr. David Riseman, Harvard University sociologist, "The ethic of the United States is in danger of becoming, 'You're a fool if you obey the rules.' "[2]

Recently in a Christian college library, I saw an empty space on a magazine shelf with a card saying, "Sorry. This periodical has been stolen." The space was for a journal of theology!

POOR IMPULSE CONTROL
FEEDS PROBLEM

The chronic refusal to say *no* grows out of poor impulse control fed by a spirit of self-indulgence. Many want all they can get as quickly as they can get it, at any cost. If barriers are in the way, they resort to anything—cheating, lying, stealing, gambling, pushing drugs, breaking up their families, and killing.

Indulgence, the disinclination to exercise restraint, is an alarming phenomenon in contemporary social relationships: parents with their children, teachers with their students, bosses with their workers, judges with criminals, and even pastors with congregations.

The end result of unchecked indulgence usually is addiction. Often our social practices become addictive, as are many of those discussed in subsequent chapters. Lawrence J. Hatterer, a medical doctor, says in his description of addiction, "There is almost always excessive use of pleasurable activities to cope with unmanageable inner conflict, pressure, stress, or confrontation."[3]

WHY LITTLE SELF-ASSERTIVENESS?

To determine why self-assertiveness has gone awry, we must look deep into our culture. The formative elements certainly include:

1. *The legacy of the social revolution of the '60s and '70s.* Although yesterday's protesters are part of today's Establishment, their spirit still lives on, both the good and the bad. Their protests against war, racial discrimination, poverty, and injustice, plus their concern for people as individuals, have enriched us all. But their emphasis upon doing what feels good—acts involving drugs, immorality, crime, and violence—in a mutual spirit of irresponsibility has scarred the soul of America.

2. *The loss of moral consensus in America.* Christian apologist Francis Schaeffer used to lament the loss of Christian consensus which once shaped the values of America. The strict court interpretation of the "no-establishment" clause in the first amendment has weakened that consensus. America's pluralism—its glory in so many ways—has led to neutralism in ideals. No longer do we have a common frame of reference, such as the Ten Commandments.

Leaders of thought, including theologian Carl F.H. Henry, attribute this breakdown to a major retrogression in public education, which has moved from specific references to the biblical God to God-in-general or a John-Doe God. "At the outset of this century," Henry says, "the instructional programs of the great Western universities frequently referred to the God of the Bible, the living, self-revealing God. Courses in moral philosophy gave prominence to the Ten Commandments and to the Sermon on the Mount, and presented Jesus of Nazareth as the perfect example of morality."[4]

This retrogression, in turn, has led to a relativistic morality given to self-assertion. Professor Bruce Hafner of Brigham Young Universiy observes: "Public school teachers have backed away from the affirmative teaching of basic principles of personal character and patriotism. School officials have been intimidated as the teaching of religious and other values have been challenged in the courts."[5]

According to Mark Cameron, administrative assistant to the Chief Justice, in 1775 religion and morals accounted for 90 percent of the material in school readers. By 1926 it had dropped to 6 percent and today is nonexistent. Cameron said references to obedience, thoughtfulness, and honesty began to disappear from third-grade readers in the '30s.[6]

Nationally, we now are losing our sense of shared values and cultural assumptions. As a result, a new generation has grown up without a public emphasis upon moral values such as honesty, integrity, thoughtfulness, nonviolence, and obedience to the law. Even at the level of higher education, William T. Bennett, chairman of the National Endowment for the Humanities, wrote as a result of its studies, "Most of our college graduates remain shortchanged in the humanities—history, literature, and philosophy, and the ideals and practices of the past that have shaped the society they enter."[7] The cohesive idealism that bonds people together is missing.

3. *Lack of discipline in the schools.* In a recent Gallup poll, parents listed lack of discipline as the number one problem in schools. Number two was drugs. Leading educators agree. The National Commission on Excellence in Education and the Twentieth Century Fund's Task Force on Education lament the general loosening of standards and discipline in schools.

The 1982 *Encyclopedia of Educational Research* concludes that "discipline has been the most troublesome problem in public education during the past two decades." As a result, nearly half of our adult population believes the growth of private schools is a good thing. And more than 10 percent of our elementary and secondary young people are enrolled in them.[8]

My own Baptist branch of the church, historically an ardent supporter of the public school system, now is experiencing one of the fastest growth rates in establishing parochial schools. In great measure this is in reaction to a lack of discipline and a failure to teach moral values in public schools.

4. *Disintegration of the family*. The nuclear family is disappearing as a major force in America. Frequent divorce, cohabitation, and alternative sexual lifestyles are playing havoc with traditional values. According to John Naisbitt, author of *Megatrends,* one of the trends shaping tomorrow's America is the shift from the family to the individual as the building block in society. In such a world, children often are left to determine their own values.[9]

For several years my daughter taught children with learning disabilities. She discovered that most of them came from broken homes and concluded that there was a direct correlation between estranged parents and disturbed children. Conversely, Sean O'Sullivan of Columbia University reported that when discipline is maintained within a family, deviant practices such as drug addiction by the children are cut in half.[10]

Family break-ups often lead to one or both separated parents indulging the children. Sometimes indulgence happens for different reasons in traditional homes. Grace and Fred Hechinger report in their book *Teenage Tyranny* that in a New York State essay contest involving 10,000 high school students, 64 percent said that parental pampering, as well as the automobile and television, made them academically and physically soft.[11]

"Of course we're soft!" confessed an eastern college coed. "We got too much too soon."

5. *Violence and terrorism in the world*. A psychic numbness, as Yale University professor of Mystical Religion, Henri Nouwen, termed it, has gripped America as a result of world violence. So much is reported in our newspapers and on television that we no

longer know how to react. Ten million people have been killed in battle since World War II.

Assassination attempts have been made on the President of the United States and the Pope. Lebanon is in shambles and Central America is a tinderbox. American government agencies have been accused of plotting the murders of foreign political leaders.

A child entering school has spent more hours watching television than he eventually will invest in four years of college. By age fifteen, according to the National Coalition on Television Violence, he or she will have seen more than 24,000 televised shootings. Under such influence, it is little wonder that children strike out to get their own way. Such violence is a manifestation of elementary social disorganization—the loss of the capacity to regulate personal behavior in the interest of others.

6. *Abandonment of the Protestant work ethic.* We've abandoned the Protestant work ethic and given way to a revival of the old Greek hedonistic ethic. For many people, life's goals are not sought in productive work which contributes to society, but in personal pleasure, leisure time activities, and self-indulgence.

We are motivated by instant success at any cost, marked by all the status symbols of having arrived. Married children want to begin where their parents left off. We must be millionaires by age forty. All of this is reinforced by slick magazines, television melodramas, and motivational lectures. In the end we are still dissatisfied and craving for more.

7. *Reaction to past legalism.* An excessive preoccupation with taboos existed at times in our past. The combined impact of Pietism, Puritanism, and Fundamentalism upon modern evangelicalism has left tracings of legalism, moralism, phariseeism, and escapism, which I deplore.

In every age the church must wrestle with the difference between legitimate biblical prohibitions and neutral cultural practices. But in reacting to old taboos, we've stereotyped the church as negative and portrayed it in much darker tones than the real situation warrants.

For example, it was said that the Puritans objected to Christians going bear hunting not because the bear would experience pain, but because Christians might enjoy pleasure.

In America, the eighteenth amendment prohibiting the manufac-
ture and sale of alcoholic beverages met with such social reaction
and lawlessness after it became effective nationally in 1920 that the
amendment was repealed in 1933. In neither the church nor the
nation do we like being told no. Our reaction to the legalism of the
past makes it difficult now for many Christians to say no to anything generally approved by our culture.

Because of these factors, the evangelical church generally has
succumbed to accommodation to its culture. No longer is any
significant behavioral difference evident between Christians and
non-Christians. Society's problems have moved into the church.
Here then is one answer to the question: "If there are so many
evangelicals in America—50 million or more—why do we not
make a bigger moral difference on the nation?" Too few Christians
are saying *no* to practices that are out of step with Scripture.

Sadly, we must confess that active churchmen were involved at
Watergate, in Congressional escapades, and Abscam and others
have been accused of dishonest practices at high levels in business.
Their personal ethics had not kept pace with their social responsibility. The sentencing judge's statement to former Environmental
Protection Agency head Rita LaVelle applies to many other government officials: "You violated a public trust."

For Christians who yielded to temptation, it was a greater violation. Unable to live by the values of an unseen kingdom to which
they professed loyalty, they were lured by the standards of a visible
nation which had lost its capacity to say no.

Doctrine and discipline—theory and practice—have been
wrenched apart. This erosion of disciplined living has been so
gradual that we are hardly aware of it, like the frog in the beaker in
the science lab.

The philosophic difference between restraint in individual life
and freedom in national life was highlighted by an editorial writer
for the sixtieth-anniversary edition of *Time* magazine (October
1983). He wrote: "Two of the great themes of the past sixty years
have been the excesses of freedom and the discovery of the need
for restraint. . . . Behind most events lay the assumption, almost a
moral imperative, that what was not free ought to be free, that
limits were intrinsically evil. To be free, in fact, seems to require an

attitude opposite that which sets one free: a sense of reasonable limitations, of self-governing restraint, the acknowledgment that one is able to escape from anything except his own skin."[12] In defining restraint, the writer acknowledges that our nation conspicuously lacks a consensus and a principle of authority.

Harvard psychiatrist Dr. Armand M. Nicholi II reaches the same conclusion, saying:

> Our society suffers from a marked inability to control basic impulses. The liberation of sexual and aggressive instincts may be due to many factors. Developments in my field, especially in psychoanalysis, may be partly responsible. Unfortunately, some people felt that freedom from sexual prohibitions would eliminate neuroses and make for a happier society. This of course has proved patently untrue.
>
> Although Freud felt that excessive suppression of instincts often leads to neuroses and accounts for much restlessness and discontent in our civilization, he also realized the danger of their liberation. When the mental counterforces which ordinarily inhibit aggression are out of action, aggression will manifest itself spontaneously and reveal man as a savage beast to whom consideration toward his own kind is something alien.[13]

Schaeffer introduced the problem of form and freedom in his film and book, *The Great Evangelical Disaster*: "Form without a balance of freedom leads to authoritarianism and to destruction of the individual. Freedom apart from form can lead to chaos and a breakdown of society."[14]

Elisabeth Elliot brings these two concepts together in her book *Discipline, the Glad Surrender*. To her, the Christian disciple uses freedom to choose to be under orders.[15] This also is Paul's concept of Christian liberty in the Book of Galatians—freedom bounded by Spirit-imposed restraints. To me, the modern application of Christian liberty calls for voluntary self-discipline under the lordship of Christ. This is the challenge evangelicals and Americans need to hear today. Freedom and restraint go hand-in-hand.

Richard Shelly Taylor defines self-discipline: "The ability to regulate conduct by principle and judgment rather than by impulse, desire, pressure or custom."[16]

The New Testament parallel for self-discipline is *egkratos—self-control,* meaning internalized self-restraint (Acts 24:25; 2 Peter 1:6). This quality is a fruit of the Holy Spirit (Gal. 5:23) and ultimately means Spirit-control. Called the Paraclete, the Holy Spirit takes His place alongside the believer to strengthen his or her ability to say no in times of temptation.

David Watson, an Anglican leader in England, concluded before his death that we cannot stand the test. Western Christians are too fat and flabby to meet the ideological challenge of our times. Watson discounted European and American Christianity as world-changing forces. He considered Third World Christianity alone strong enough to compete against the two rival forces of Marxism and Islam. In the Third World, Christian commitment hammered out on the anvil of oppression, injustice, and poverty has become the church's most powerful expression.[17]

SPIRITUAL STAMINA NEEDED

I believe the West can be stronger. But we need spiritual stamina to dig in our heels and say *no* in the face of temptation. Evangelical churches still have time to mobilize a contingent of resolute people who refuse, as Bible translator J.B. Phillips puts it, to "be squeezed into this world's mold" (Rom. 12:2, PH) and who by their lifestyle confront their culture.

The secular world is full of support organizations: AA (Alcoholics Anonymous), MADD (Mothers Against Drunk Drivers), SMILES (Sexually Molested Individuals Lending Earnest Support), Tough Love (parents confronting youth rebellion), Neighborhood Alert (citizens on watch for criminals), SADD (Students Against Drunk Driving), and SPARK (School Prevention of Addiction through Rehabilitation and Knowledge). Each of these groups is helping people say no. Surely our churches can do the same.

After years of listening to college chapel talks, a professor friend of mine plaintively commented: "I get frustrated hearing each day about high spiritual goals and great ideas. What I need is someone to point out the next single small step forward I can take."

In subsequent chapters, I suggest seven small steps we can take to say a big *no* to the debilitating forces in our culture.

THE GLASS OF WINE

"Elizabeth! What a funny place to wind up together! Who would have thought forty years ago that we'd meet here?" Movie actor Peter Lawford greeted Elizabeth Taylor in 1983 at the center for drug addiction and alcoholism sponsored by former First Lady Betty Ford in the Eisenhower Medical Center at Rancho Mirage, California.

The two hadn't seen each other since they'd worked on the films *The White Cliffs of Dover* and *Little Women*. Now they both were patients trying to overcome chemical addiction.

"I was just drinking too much and got sick of it. Never again! I began to see the direction my life was going and decided then and there to check into Eisenhower. It's the smartest thing I've done in ages. What a wonderful feeling I have now," Peter told her, smiling widely.¹ But Lawford may have been too late. Less than a year later he was dead, at age 61.

Never again! What a forceful expression for our times and for people of all ages. Particularly, I would encourage Christian leaders shaping our new generation of young people to help them avoid the trauma of a detoxification center by saying to liquor, *"Never again!"* if they drink. And for those who do not drink, encourage them to affirm: "I will never *start*!"

When I say "never again" or "never start," I include the whole

19

range of alcoholic beverages: distilled whiskey with its 40-50 percent alcohol content, dessert wine with its 17-20 percent, dinner
wine with its 12 percent, and beer with 4 percent—anything with
ethyl alcohol (ethanol) which causes intoxication.

WHAT THE BIBLE SAYS

The Bible sets a precedent for taking a strong
stance against alcoholic beverages, although sometimes these
Scripture passages are overlooked. For example, Judges 13 tells of
Samson's mother before she was to bear a son. An angel came to
guide her through her pregnancy so that Samson would grow to be
the man God envisioned.

"You are sterile and childless, but you are going to conceive and
have a son. Now see to it that you drink no wine or other
fermented drink and that you do not eat anything unclean," the
angel said to her (Jud. 13:3-4). Thus, during her pregnancy Samson's mother was to say *no* to the wine of the Old Testament.

The Book of Daniel opens with the illuminating story of a king
who wanted to compare the captive Israelite young men with the
youth of his kingdom to see which were superior. He assigned
them daily food and wine from his own table in a three-year
training program to enter his service. "But Daniel resolved not to
defile himself with the royal food and wine, and he asked the chief
official for permission not to defile himself this way" (Dan. 1:8).
During the long training period, Daniel said, "I will not drink
wine."

Abstinence was a lifelong practice for John the Baptist. An angel
said to his mother, "He will be a joy and delight to you, and many
will rejoice because of his birth, for he will be great in the sight of
the Lord. He is never to take wine or other fermented drink, and he
will be filled with the Holy Spirit even from birth" (Luke 1:14-15).

While Samson's mother practiced abstinence during her pregnancy and Daniel during a training period in a limited teetotalism,
John's was lifelong abstinence. He shared this vow with other
Nazarites whose nonalcoholic way of life was a vital part of their
dedication to God.

Total abstinence is universalized by the Apostle Paul in Romans
14—the passage devoted to dynamic principles about Christian

living, Christian liberty, Christian sensitivity to the conscience of others, and Christian devotion to God.

Paul concludes: "Do not destroy the work of God for the sake of food. All food is clean, but it is wrong for a man to eat anything that causes someone else to stumble. It is better not to eat meat or drink wine or to do anything else that will cause your brother to fall" (Rom. 14:20-21). Here he extends the principle of abstinence by teaching that it is desirable never to drink wine or eat food offered to idols if your Christian liberty causes someone else to stumble.

LEADERS SOFT ON ABSTINENCE

Today too few are heeding this teaching. Seldom do you hear, "I'll never start!" You have to go to the Bible, to meetings of Alcoholics Anonymous, or to detoxification centers to hear people say of alcohol, "Never again!"

In my boyhood days, my church observed every thirteenth Sunday as Temperance Sunday. The Sunday School lesson that morning always was devoted to teaching abstinence. We have long since given up the special emphasis of the thirteenth Sunday. And we have long since given up preaching sermons on abstinence. Why?

In part, many Christian leaders—respected, earnest, evangelical men and women of God—do not think total abstinence ought to be taught in the twentieth century. They feel emphasis should be placed on our liberty in Christ, which includes freedom to drink alcoholic beverages, at least in moderation. I respect their reasoning, even though I dissent from it. Sadly, they say nothing about abstinence and very little about moderation.

Other leaders say nothing about the use of alcohol because to them it is only one of many possible weaknesses. Why talk about just this particular problem? There are worse sins of the flesh than drinking alcoholic beverages, even if they do cause drunkenness. Certainly sins of the spirit can be worse. These leaders argue that the Bible talks about *all* sins. So why single out one? As a result, they say little or nothing about alcohol and all too often fail to mention any sins of the flesh. These are all virtually lost in the silence of the church. Sometimes we say nothing about alcohol because we're painfully aware of our own shortcomings. Intemperance may not be our problem, but we have others. Living in our glass houses, we don't want to throw stones at people who might hurl them back.

In my boyhood church in Sioux Falls, South Dakota, an old Swede who was a strong pillar in the church smoked big, black cigars. Though loved and respected by everyone, he occasionally was chided for his smelly habit. Always he had the same answer: "Well, that's my sin. What's yours?" His reply usually silenced his critics.

For twenty-eight years I saw an increasing number of young people come to Bethel College and Seminary from the finest evangelical churches in our country. Yet few had very little conviction about the problems caused by alcoholic beverages. One of my most difficult roles as president was to advise some students to drop out to rethink their lifestyle. I felt they needed to decide if they really wanted to study in a setting where total abstinence was a stipulation for community living. The number of such students is greater today and growing. Because they come from fine evangelical churches, I address the issue of alcohol with growing concern.

WHAT ABOUT MODERATION?

As an advocate of total abstinence, I'm usually asked the question, "Doesn't the Bible actually teach moderation in the use of alcohol, not total abstinence?"

I've looked critically at the New Testament on this point, having done my Master of Theology work in New Testament Greek under Dr. W.W. Adams, a great scholar and teacher of Koiné Greek. My dissertation was based upon an intensive study of *oinos*, the Greek word for wine used in Paul's pastoral epistles.

The word *oinos* occurs alone only twenty-nine times in the entire New Testament and five other times as part of compound words. In the pastoral epistles it occurs five times. In each instance, Paul refers to wine as he counsels Timothy and Titus regarding their leadership roles in the church. These instances make it clear that Paul approved of some use of wine by people in the churches pastored by Timothy and Titus.

He instructs: "If anyone sets his heart on being an overseer (a bishop or pastor), he desires a noble task. Now the overseer must be above reproach, the husband of but one wife, temperate, self-controlled, respectable, hospitable, able to teach, *not given to much wine*" (1 Tim. 3:1-2, emphasis added).

Certainly, Paul appears to be counseling Timothy to allow church leaders to drink wine but not too much. He also says, "Deacons, likewise, are to be men worthy of respect, sincere, *not indulging in much wine,* and not pursuing dishonest gain" (1 Tim. 3:8, emphasis added). So for both deacons and pastors, it is permissible to use wine.

He also counsels Timothy himself, advising, "Stop drinking only water, and use a little wine because of your stomach and your frequent illnesses" (1 Tim. 5:23). Timothy at least was allowed the medicinal use of wine.

When Paul advises Titus about the role of overseer, he writes: "Since an overseer is entrusted with God's work, he must be blameless—not overbearing, not quick-tempered, *not given to much wine*" (Titus 1:7, emphasis added). He tells Titus and Timothy the same thing about the conduct of bishops and overseers—they are to drink wine moderately.

When Paul talks about church women, he says, "Likewise, teach the older women to be reverent in the way they live, not to be slanderers or *addicted to much wine*" (Titus 2:3, emphasis added).

Obviously, Paul is instructing his young disciples to encourage their people to be moderate in using *oinos.* Don't drink too much. Don't become addicted!

Does *oinos* in the New Testament refer to fermented or unfermented wine? This is still a live question for many Christians. But few Greek scholars teach that the wine used in Bible days was unfermented. In my judgment, *oinos* in the New Testament and its parallel words in Hebrew in the Old Testament mean fermented wine. One can deduce this from the derivation of the word *oinos* and also because in the New Testament no reference is made to a process to keep wine from fermenting. As soon as grapes were harvested, people pressed out the juice by walking barefoot on them in large, hollowed-out rocks serving as vats; the wine began almost immediately to ferment. So much action was in the fermentation that for forty days the wine couldn't be put in leather wineskins. Once in wineskins, it could be kept for as long as three years. By then, it was no longer good wine. There was no refrigeration—no place for cooling wine to stop the fermenting process. The very fact that the process couldn't be stopped is an indication the fruit of the vine very quickly became fermented.

The Bible's many warnings about drunkenness certainly are another indication that wine made people drunk. "Be not drunk with wine, wherein is excess; but be filled with the Spirit" (Eph. 5:18, KJV) is a very familiar admonition to us. All through his epistles, Paul warns against drunkenness, even at the Lord's table. He acknowledges that wine causes drunkenness.

One custom during Bible times is still another indication that the wine was fermented. At festive banquets the governor of the feast monitored wine-drinking to keep it from becoming excessive. At the feast of Cana of Galilee, where Jesus performed His first miracle, the governor of the feast noticed right away that the last wine was better than the first.

In light of Paul's counsel about wine, many people understandably conclude that moderation in using alcoholic beverages is the New Testament standard. Since Paul counseled, "Don't drink *too* much wine," and not, "Don't drink wine," then our modern principle should be moderation, this school of thought suggests.

LOCAL CUSTOM AND UNIVERSAL PRINCIPLE

However, as most students of Scripture know, there is a difference between a local custom and a universal principle. One of the great challenges of biblical interpretation is to determine whether a custom is only a local, time-bound practice or if it is meant to be universalized as a principle for all Christians in all times. This is especially true in the pastoral epistles in which, besides drunkenness, Paul refers to such social issues as slavery and the submissive role of women.

For example, slavery is discussed in 1 Timothy 6:1: "All who are under the yoke of slavery should consider their masters worthy of full respect, so that God's name and our teaching may not be slandered." Nowhere in the New Testament does Paul teach rebellion, striking, fighting for rights, or defending human dignities.

Freedom is a new concept in the Gospel, and Paul encourages everyone to begin with the Gospel. He sent Onesimus, the runaway slave he had led to Christ, back to his master, Philemon, saying that Onesimus should be welcomed not as a slave but as a brother beloved in the Lord.

When Paul was writing that letter, a third of the Roman Empire was in slavery. Slaves were not distinguished by the color of their skin but sometimes could be recognized by the holes bored in their ears. Generally, slaves looked just like free people. They had become slaves as captives of war or were pirated on the high seas and sold into slavery. Some were born into slavery. One of every three people in the Roman Empire was a slave.

Paul could easily have instigated a social revolution. Instead, he advised slaves to be obedient—to stay under the yoke—and to consider their masters with respect. That's his consistent word in all the epistles.

Was he condoning slavery? No. But he urged slaves to bring credit to the new Gospel of Jesus Christ which he was proclaiming. The universal principle was to bring honor and glory to Jesus Christ. The local application for slaves was that they perform their service well.

Ultimately, the Gospel—with difficulty—led to emancipation for slaves and to equality. We no longer suggest that people should be slaves and obedient to masters. We do, however, urge that people bring honor and glory to Christ in their vocations.

Paul taught in a similar way about the role of women. In 1 Timothy 2:11-15 he says, "A woman should learn in quietness and full submission. I do not permit a woman to teach or to have authority over a man; she must be silent. For Adam was formed first, then Eve. And Adam was not the one deceived; it was the woman who was deceived and became a sinner. But women will be kept safe through childbirth, if they continue in faith, love, and holiness with propriety." In similar passages, Paul also discusses submission and silence.

Today we do not insist that women be silent in church. This is not the *universal* principle. In Paul's world, a woman who spoke out in public reflected insubordination in the family and often was involved in immoral living. Thus, in first-century culture, it was more becoming to the brand new Gospel for a woman to be silent in church.

The *universal* principle is not silence but an orderly relationship within family life. However one interprets the universal principle—and there are all kinds of applications—the local principle that women keep silent in church is not applicable to our day. The local practice is not meant to be the universal principle.

The point is what was a local practice in one culture is not necessarily appropriate for honoring Christ in another culture. The role of biblical hermeneutics is to extract from local practices the universal principles to be applied elsewhere. So in these passages in the pastoral epistles, the universal principle is that bishops, deacons, and older women—as well as Titus and Timothy—be irreproachable in conduct.

In that first-century water-short culture, irreproachable conduct meant moderate use of the primary beverage—unfortified, natural wine. Because rain occurred only part of the year, the water supply was insufficient. Consequently, water was stored in wells and cisterns. However, the water became dirty and bacteria and sediment developed. For drinking purposes, the wine was combined with three parts water, greatly reducing its alcoholic content. While this practice was not followed in Old Testament times, it was true throughout the New Testament.

The abundance of vineyards in the wine-growing country made the use of wine natural. But in spite of the fact the wine was diluted, its addictive qualities caused some people to drink immoderately and often become drunk. So Paul reminded Christians to keep their conduct irreproachable before God. That called for restricted use of wine. But the moderate use of such diluted wine in New Testament times is altogether different from the moderate use of twentieth-century wine.

WHAT ABOUT TODAY?

What then is the principle for today? In my judgment, the universal ideal is irreproachable conduct with regard to alcoholic beverages. I believe that total abstinence carries out this principle more faithfully than moderation in our culture. So to the question: "Doesn't the New Testament teach moderation?" I answer yes—*as a local practice for that time*. But it is not necessarily a universal principle for all time.

A second question I'm often asked is: "What's wrong with taking just a single glass of wine?" Unfortunately, wine drinking is the point of greatest softness among youth growing up in our evangelical churches. Some of my friends say wine has valuable benefits. They tell me it gives them a sense of relaxation after a busy day and a heightened feeling of sociability. Wine reduces inhibitions as the brain center comes under the control of stimulants and users talk more easily. Aid to digestion also is frequently mentioned as an advantage. My friends who drink also say that an alcoholic beverage helps them forget problems for a time.

FOUR REASONS FOR ABSTINENCE

On the negative side, however, four reasons stand out to me for observing the principle of irreproachable conduct by total abstinence from wine and all other alcoholic beverages, except when prescribed medically:

1. *One drink leads to more.* Herbert Hills, executive director of Alcohol Problems Association in Seattle, insists that of every three persons who start as social drinkers, one ends as a problem drinker. How can anyone be moderate using a narcotic when its first function is to call for more?

The *first* drink has led 68 percent of all Americans over age 18 to use alcohol to some extent. Thus, any church which teaches total abstinence must run counter to more than two-thirds of the American population—and perhaps to the same percentage listening to the Sunday sermon. A Gallup survey indicated that 66 percent of all teenagers are involved in some drinking. A University of Michigan national study of teenagers revealed that 34 percent of all twelfth-graders used alcohol twenty or more times during the twelve months preceding the study. A total of 1.3 million teenagers are afflicted with serious drinking problems. An estimated 90 percent of America's 12 million college students drink liquor. Fifty percent are heavy drinkers if not problem drinkers. Many, in fact, are alcoholics.

One encouraging aspect of evangelicalism, according to a Gallup poll, is that while one-fourth of the nation abstains from using alcohol, two-thirds of all evangelical Christians abstain. While half of all clergy abstain from alcohol, three-fourths of all evangelical clergy abstain. Whatever else is true, a discernible base of support for total abstinence still exists in the evangelical wing of the church and can make a difference in our nation today.

One drink leads to another by stages: the occasional drinker, the regular social drinker, the alcohol-dependent drinker who drinks as a solution to problems, the addictive drinker who deliberately stops for a drink on the way home from work, and the alcoholic drinker. One drink *does* lead to another.

An old Japanese proverb says:

> *First the man takes a drink,*
> *Then the drink takes a drink,*
> *And then the drink takes the man.*

This can begin with beer, lowest in alcoholic content among American beverages. Ansley Cuddingham Moore, a counselor writing in *Christian Century*, noted: "I include beer and wine in my call for abstinence because there are addicts who never touch stronger beverages. A would-be suicide who never drank anything but beer was recently pulled from a river. Beer had dulled his senses.

One of my own acquaintances drinks only beer, comes home at night, and when he has consumed a large enough quantity will do violence to his wife. Cases of this kind have driven me as a counselor to oppose the use of beer and wine; they do much harm to people and they are frequently the stepping-stones to both whiskey and drugs."[2]

Cynthia Parsons, a reporter for the *Christian Science Monitor*, comments: "Drink responsibly? What rot! It is irresponsible to drink!"[3]

Betty Ford, reviewing her personal victory in overcoming alcoholism, wrote: "In our society we get to know one another over drinks. We associate feasts and celebrations with liquor. We think we have to drink, that it's a social necessity. . . .It's romantic as long as you can handle it—for years I could and did—but it's misery when you become addicted."[4]

In the future, the one-drink-leads-to-another syndrome will become an even greater problem. One national corporation, formerly only producing soft drinks, is beginning a concerted campaign to double wine consumption in the next decade.[5] Our use of wine already is growing at a rate of 6 or 7 percent a year. This company and others hope to increase our annual per capita consumption of wine from 2.2 gallons a person to 5 gallons. They plan to accomplish this by selling wine through fast-food chains. They are just beginning their propaganda barrage. Anyone who says no to alcohol is going to have to fight against tremendous pressures.

During my senior year in high school, I represented my school in state and national oratorical contests. My high-school oration was entitled "Liquor Propaganda and Youth." My thesis was that whether you're for or against liquor, you ought to be against the insidious and distorted propaganda used to promote it. I gave that speech more than forty years ago. Since then nothing has changed, and the propaganda pressures in the future will be even greater. America is now spending $40 billion a year to promote the use of alcohol—$250 for every individual in the nation—and that amount will increase as advertising is intensifed.

2. *One drink encourages others to drink.* We never know who can or can't handle alcohol.

In an article entitled "Why Teens Drink," published by the National Institute on Alcohol Education and reprinted by the Pittsburgh Press, young people listed five reasons for their social drinking:

a. My parents drink.
b. We had drinking problems in our family and I got caught up in them.
c. There was an absence of affection in my family.
d. I had feelings of personal inferiority.
e. My friends drink and I felt pressured.

Three of these five reasons for drinking grew out of the drinking habits of others. If you're a Christian seeking to be sensitive to other people, it is helpful to remember that one drink on your part may lead another to begin a practice he can't control. You are your brother's keeper.

This responsibility needs to be emphasized even in church

practices. Recently, a seminary student told me how deeply involved with alcohol he used to be. "It began," he said, "in my church at social functions. I actually learned to drink in church!" One drink led to another until he was on the brink of alcoholism. At a critical point, he met God in a life-changing spiritual encounter, found victory over his habit, and offered his life to God for the ministry. His fellow church members probably never knew how close they came to destroying his life. In West Germany, Baptists passed a denomination-wide policy to change their historic practice of serving fermented wine at Communion services to serving only unfermented grape juice. From bitter experience, they had learned that recovered alcoholics often were led back into their old life by participating in the Lord's Supper at church services. Surely, of all places, we are to be our brother's keeper in church.

3. *One drink can lead to deep personal tragedy.* The first glass of an alcoholic beverage could be the first step toward heavy drinking. Personal tragedy may then result, taking the form of physical damage to your body—cirrhosis of the liver, diseased kidneys, increased blood pressure, inflammation of the stomach lining, destruction of blood platelets, and a permanent deposit in the brain known as the THG factor, not unlike that produced by heroin. Other possible deleterious side affects from additives in wine may result, according to recent reports. Eighty different substances are used to filter, clarify, or stabilize wine. Residue, such as sulfur dioxide, may remain in wine with potential harm to some people. The result is physical damage to the body, meant to be maintained by believers as the sacred temple of the Holy Spirit.

Another personal tragedy is alcoholism itself. Ten million alcoholics—which is 10 percent of all American drinkers—have crossed the line and can't control their drinking any longer. They drink alone, they drink often, and they drink profusely; they tend to hide their liquor supply, and their minds often dwell on drinking during the day. They've developed an increased tolerance which allows them to drink even more. But they've become alcoholics. They can't stop drinking.

Besides these 10 million, another 10 million are being treated for the *symptoms* of alcoholism. They are close to the brink but not quite there. Among these number are the 1.3 million teenagers who have drinking problems. Five percent of them are already alcoholics. When some mix drugs with alcohol, as many entertainers have done, alcoholism can be fatal. An average of 10 percent of U.S. alcoholics ultimately commit suicide.

A lesser-known tragedy is FAS—Fetal Alcoholic Syndrome. When a pregnant woman takes a drink, she also is giving the liquor to her fetus. That's because alcohol, unlike food, is quickly absorbed into the body's system. Within seconds, 80 percent of the alcohol is in the bloodstream going to all parts of the body, including the fetus.

A child born to an alcoholic mother is 10 percent more likely to have a deformity or some other physical problem. Fetal Alcoholic Syndrome is the third leading cause of birth defects. Each year 2,000 children are born with physical impairments due to alcohol in their mother's body.

Still another personal tragedy is the befuddled mind. The minimum concentration of alcohol in the bloodstream to indicate drunkenness usually is .10 percent. That danger point is reached quickly. A six-ounce glass of wine, twelve-ounce can of beer, or one-and-a-half ounce cup of eighty proof whiskey are all equivalent in alcoholic content. Three cans of beer will dangerously affect the driving ability of a 160-pound person. Some say one can of beer will affect anyone's ability to drive well. Carried further, consider the possible effect of alcohol on strategic decision-making in government, business, or in military maneuvers.

4. *One drink can unlock the door to a Pandora's box of social ills.* These include among workers lowered productivity, absenteeism, hangovers, inefficient work, Monday morning blues, and returning home with a headache. All of this costs American industry an estimated $43 billion a year. In a time when America already is losing the productivity race to Japan, Korea, Hong Kong, Taiwan, and even to Mexico, we ought to do everything possible to become more productive—not less. An estimated 10 percent of executives and professionals in industrial nations suffer from alcohol abuse—5 percent worldwide lose 25 percent of their productivity.[7]

Many nations have adopted the old Puritan work ethic we once had, while we've switched to the Greek pleasure ethic. Perhaps the best definition I've heard of the Puritan work ethic is: an inner compulsion to do your best regardless of your pay. That no longer is the American spirit and, consequently, we're losing out internationally. Alcohol is a contributing factor.

Accidental death is another social evil in Pandora's box. Fifty percent of all automobile accidents are due to alcohol consumption by at least one of the drivers. As a result, alcohol-dulled drivers kill 25,000 people every year on our highways. During the Vietnamese War, 57,000 Americans died and our youth protested violently. But during the same period, few raised their voices when 75,000 Americans died in alcohol-related tragedies on our highways and streets.

One person is killed every twenty-three minutes as a result of drunk driving. A driver who had killed an eleven-year-old bicyclist said, "I couldn't see him when I was drunk. But I can see him now. I remember!"

While you know these statistics, you may not be aware that nearly 50 percent of falling, fire, and drowning deaths are also caused by alcohol in the victim. A sheriff estimated that 80 percent of all boating accidents on a famous Minnesota lake are caused by drinking pilots. The Coast Guard insists that drunk boating is more dangerous than drunk driving and that drunk swimming is more dangerous than drunk walking.

STILL MORE REASONS FOR ABSTINENCE

Still another social evil resulting from alcohol is divorce. Dr. Richard Heilman, director of the chemical dependency program at Veterans Hospital in Minneapolis, estimates that one-half of all divorces in America are related to alcohol. Another related evil is family violence and abuse.

Organized crime is another evil connected with alcohol. We used to say that Prohibition created bootleggers and increased crime in America. However, liquor is related to far more crime today. In Dade County, Florida, for example, 25 percent of all bars and restaurants are reputed to be in the hands of the Mafia. Fighting, prostitution, and drugs are common in these businesses. A while ago a *Miami Herald* headline declared: "Liquor Trade Out of Control."[6] But the underworld moved in and now controls it.

Government agencies now spend $300 billion annually to correct problems caused by alcohol abuse in America. For every dollar our government receives from liquor taxes, it spends $11 to repair the damage caused by the sales.

What's wrong with drinking one glass of wine? One glass can lead to another. One glass can encourage others to drink and go further. One glass will lead many into deep personal tragedy. One glass may open the door to a Pandora's box of social evils.

All of these problems were illustrated vividly by Asa Bushnell in eighteen years of downward mobility on the corporate ladder. At age twenty-six, he occupied an influential position as public relations director for New Jersey's attorney general. But nothing seemed as important to him as the next drink. And those next drinks led to a bumpy employment ride—to police reporting, to writing for a weekly paper, to cab driving, to a three-month whirl with the *Phoenix Gazette*, and finally to a ghetto curbside in Los Angeles. "As I sat there sharing an ill-gotten bottle of cheap wine with three newly acquired soul brothers, the question crossed my muddled mind, 'What's an Ivy League college graduate doing in this predicament?' "[8] He had touched bottom. There a friend discovered him and guided him to Alcoholics Anonymous, where he made a remarkable transition back to sobriety and usefulness. But nearly two decades of his life had been wasted.

Against all of this background, it seems to me that it is not correct to say that the New Testament teaches moderation in using alcohol for twentieth-century America. The New Testament calls for Christians to be circumspect, to set a good example, to be irreproachable, and to refuse to be squeezed into the world's mold. Such a call establishes a credible base for total abstinence from alcohol, including even a glass of wine.

One commentator defined temperance—a New Testament fruit of the Spirit—as: "Moderation in that which is good and total abstinence from that which is evil." In light of alcohol's effects upon America, I believe alcohol is an insidious beverage, and our best response to it is total abstinence.

Other important principles in the New Testament govern the use of wine. One concerns *enslavement*: "All things are lawful for me; but I will not be brought under the power of any" (1 Cor. 6:12, ASV). Another principle concerns *edification*: "All things are lawful, but not all things edify" (1 Cor. 10:23, ASV). Paul is saying, "I will not do anything which will not build me up in body, mind, heart or soul." The third principle concerns *sensitivity*: "If what I eat causes my brother to fall into sin, I will never eat meat again" (1 Cor. 8:13). If the principle of moderation is put side by side with the principles of enslavement, edification, and sensitivity, perhaps many Christians then would respond as Peter Lawford did: *"Never again!"* and many would never even start drinking.

ESTABLISH YOUR CUTTING LINE

What I am calling for is a conservative cutting line in social practice. Wherever you establish your cutoff point for the use of alcohol, you will have to battle to keep it there. What do you say about your cutting line? "I'll only drink beer at a ball game."/"I'll drink champagne at festive occasions or if the airline stewardess offers it to me."/ "I'll have a dinner drink with friends at home, but go no further."/ "I'll have a drink with friends in a cocktail lounge once in a while."/ "I'll drink hard liquor occasionally."/ "I enjoy getting drunk once in a while, but never more than two or three times a year."

Where do you draw your cutting line? You will have to fight to keep it there. Your instincts, peer pressure, business, stress, family problems, and the national media will encourage you to keep moving that cutoff point toward increasingly greater use of alcoholic beverages. If you are going to have to fight anyway, why not draw the line at the most conservative point—total abstinence—and fight your battle there?

T H R E E

DRUG ABUSE

During a spiritual renewal conference in Colombia, South America, I learned from a missionary translator that American cocaine buyers had almost decimated his ministry in the mountains. He had worked patiently with a small tribe learning their oral language, creating a written vocabulary, and translating portions of Scripture to teach them to read. Then he began translating the Scriptures to provide the people with the entire Bible. Although they had shown interest in the project, none had accepted Christ.

Finally after twelve years, the Bible translation was completed and printed. It was another step in fulfilling Wycliffe founder Cameron Townsend's vision for getting the Gospel into 1,000 village languages. But when the missionary flew in to present his labor of love to the tribe, not one person showed up!

During the missionary's absence, cocaine buyers had come and offered the poor Indians what seemed fabulous prices for cocoa leaves they grew in abundance. Since then, everyone was far from the village working feverishly among their plants. Nothing else mattered. The lure of money from the illicit drug trade had supplanted everything else. Not even the Bible in their own tongue was important anymore. No one cared. The missionary returned to the jungle base station, discouraged and defeated.

Of course, the story is not ended. Sometime, somehow God will vindicate His Word, and it will not return void but will accomplish what He pleases. As for the Indians, they are not to blame. Poor, exploited, and ignorant, they unwittingly had become pawns of the drug Mafia. They had grown cocoa leaves all their lives, chewing the leaves for mild stimulation—much as Americans get from coffee. Now they were being *paid* for raising as much as they could as quickly as possible. Who could blame them? Innocently, these tribal Indians are the sources of supply for most of the cocaine sold on the streets of America's major cities.

They remain unaware that their cocoa leaves are sold for hundreds of times the small amount of money paid them. Through processors and then along many devious routes around the world, their crop reaches New York and Los Angeles, and cities in-between. People hooked on cocaine pay $100 to $125 per gram to satisfy their habit, making the leaves sold by the Indians for a pittance more valuable than gold.

Little do the Indians know about the politics of drugs involving the United States and the Andean governments of Colombia, Bolivia, and Peru—the three major sources of cocaine. These governments' attempts to destroy cocoa plantings and dry up the trade at the source are largely unsuccessful. Nor do the Indians know about the "mules"—the people who would do anything to transport the drug into America for a price.

One common technique used by drug smugglers to pass by custom inspectors unnoticed involves their swallowing a powder-filled balloon and later eliminating it. Some, however, have experienced horrible deaths when the balloons have broken inside their bodies, releasing lethal doses of cocaine. But for big money these smugglers are willing to take big risks.

Even John DeLorean, wonder-worker of the auto world, was accused and tried for being a conduit for $24 million worth of illegal cocaine—ostensibly to shore up a toppling financial empire.[1] Although he was exonerated, his case is a reminder that thousands of people are innocently or otherwise involved in the huge $110 billion trade in illicit drugs in America. By comparison, the $500 million spent by law enforcement agencies to fight drugs is simply inadequate.

SOLUTION NO SIMPLE TASK

Many thoughtful political leaders believe that our nation will never stop illegal trafficking in drugs. In a special report to the *New York Times*, Joel Brinkley observed gloomily:

> Some people doubt that the world can ever solve the problem of illicit drug production. For a century, drug traffickers have outwitted or evaded almost every drug-control strategy tried. In country after country, they bribe scores of public officials. They turn drug-producing regions into autonomous armed camps. They lure so many citizens into the illicit drug trade that local and national economies become hopelessly reliant upon the easy narco-dollars.[2]

The unpleasant fact is, as Attorney General William French Smith has pointed out, that unless the demand for drugs is eliminated, the money to be gained from the illegal sale of drugs is so great that dealers will continue to take whatever risks are necessary.

One possible hopeful sign on the horizon is that the government of Colombia has declared war on its drug traffickers. There, 400 miles southeast of Bogota, you will find the largest cocaine processing plant in the world. But when Colombia's justice minister was murdered by the drug Mafia in April 1984, President Cuartes declared war and insisted that "there will be no truce for drug traffickers. There will be punishment without mercy."[3] His sweeping reform of the bureaucracy may eventually remove as many as 400 judges and 280 policemen suspected of drug complicity. If successful, his crusade may stem some of the flow of Colombian drugs into the United States.

At the same time, however, our neighbor Cuba seems to not only allow but to encourage drug smugglers from Colombia and other countries to unload shipments and refuel their boats and planes in Cuba. This is the conclusion of Francis Mullen, the head of the Drug Enforcement Administration. "The Cuban government has two purposes," he told a congressional panel. "It wants to damage American society by aiding drug pushers, and it raises revenues from the smugglers to help finance terrorist activities in South and Central America."[4]

THE NEED TO UNDERSTAND

This indicates that drugs will continue to be a major problem for years to come. Hence, Christians need to understand its nature if the church is to reinforce the government in this struggle for the very soul of our nation.

Besides cocaine and heroin, many other drugs on the black market since the social revolt of the '60s have been abused in America. However, the legitimate uses for both natural and synthetic drugs sometimes make it difficult to draw the line between medical and sensual use.

I am indebted to Dr. Hardin B. Jones, professor of medical physics and physiology at the University of California, Berkeley, and nutritionist Helen Jones for a helpful delineation of sensual drugs as "those the body doesn't need but which give a strong sense of pleasure."[5]

Dr. Melvin H. Weinswig, associate dean of the School of Pharmacy, University of Wisconsin, places sensual drugs into five categories:[6]

1. *Stimulants.* Exciting part of the nervous system, these include cocaine and the similar but less-potent amphetamines: benzedrine, dexedrine, and methydrine—known on the street as bennies, dexies, and speed. Two socially accepted stimulants are nicotine and caffeine. Nicotine now is recognized by the U.S. government as harmful, and a statement known to most Americans is required on cigarette packages and advertising: "Warning: The Surgeon General Has Determined That Cigarette Smoking Is Dangerous to Your Health." The second, caffeine, currently is raising serious questions.

2. *Narcotics.* Rather than exciting the system, these produce insensibility or stupor because of their depressant effect. Narcotic drugs are derived from opium-producing poppies, largely grown in Turkey, Iran, Egypt, and India, and appear in the form of heroin, morphine, and codeine.

Narcotics are often combined with stimulants. For example, cocaine (which excites) and heroin (which sedates) are commonly combined, subjecting the human body to an inner tension similar to simultaneously depressing both the accelerator and brake of an automobile.

3. *Depressants*. Another group of tranquilizers act primarily on basic personality traits, exaggerating both the good and bad and leading to physical dependence. These include alcohol and a group of barbiturates commonly known to drug addicts as red devils, yellow jackets, and rainbows.

4. *Hallucinogens*. The use of these illegal drugs leads to distortion of perception, dream images, and hallucinations. Among them are LSD (lysergic acid diethylamide), PCP (angel dust), and mescaline. Marijuana also is considered a hallucinogen, producing relaxation or excitement and possible impairment of judgment and coordination.

5. *Synthetic and refined chemicals*. A fifth category of chemicals misused by many consist of such innocent substances as glue, gasoline, and paint thinner. When a person sniffs fumes from these, drunkenness and serious physical damage to the liver and kidneys can result.

MAJOR DRUGS OF THE '80S

Of all the drugs listed, three are emerging as the drugs of the '80s. Two are the popular hallucinogens PCP (angel dust) and marijuana. The third is cocaine, the drug of the affluent. Each has made a large-scale penetration of American life at every level.

According to former Illinois Senator Charles Percy, PCP (Phencyclidine) has become such a popular drug that the problem now is of epidemic proportions. For millions, PCP has supplanted LSD, once described by drug guru Timothy Leary as a mental vitamin that everyone should take.

Commonly known as angel dust, the white powder is cheap to produce and readily available. Users generally make up a mixture of PCP with another substance, roll it in a leaf, and smoke it. The drug's effect is similar to LSD, producing feelings of strength, power, and invulnerability, together with a dreamy sense of estrangement. PCP's effects on the central nervous system are devastating, often leading to acute psychosis, violence, coma, cardiac arrest, bizarre behavior, hallucinations, mood disorders, and paranoia.

Alfred Russell of the Federal Drug Enforcement Administration says of PCP: "I can't think of a more vicious drug. I can't condemn it enough."

In a recent year nearly 250 young people died from PCP, some jumping from tall buildings and others striding into the ocean. One man in his delusion pulled out all his teeth with a pair of pliers without feeling pain. In spite of the damaging results, more than 7 million people have used this animal tranquilizer on themselves in their quest for hallucinatory experiences.

Some people believe that drug abuse is no longer the fad it was in the '60s and '70s, but instead it is an enduring way of life in the '80s.

Milder forms of the PCP experience can be found in marijuana, another sometimes-hallucinogenic drug. Twenty-five percent of the American population—54 million people—are believed to have tried marijuana. And probably 23 million smoke it regularly, according to the National Institute on Drug Abuse. Second only to alcohol in popularity, marijuana use fortunately is declining among high school youth.

Each year Americans smoke 10,000 tons of marijuana, worth about $20 billion. Often referred to as a recreational drug, it is used by many as a communal drug to enhance their sense of loving relationships with friends. Others find in it euphoria and relaxation.

Marijuana has been the most controversial of all illegal drugs. Many efforts have been made to decriminalize it, and in some states possessing modest amounts of marijuana is no longer a crime. Recent evidence, however, confirms that marijuana is far from harmless. The president of the American Council on Marijuana, Dr. Robert L. DuPont, has concluded that the drug has most of the negative health effects of alcohol and tobacco, as well as unique dangers all its own.[7]

And Dr. Gabriel Nahas, research professor of anesthesiology of the College of Physicians and Surgeons of Columbia University, reports that the cumulative effect of marijuana is harmful to the body because of its potential for disrupting cell chemistry.

Marijuana also adversely affects the reproductive system, the pulmonary function of the lungs, and the brain center—leading to changes in mood, short-term memory loss, impairment of motor skills, and, with high doses, hallucinations. While these effects were not known when smoking pot first became widespread, they are being reinforced regularly by subsequent research.[8]

Most sobering is the changed perspective of Dr. DuPont, who in 1974 insisted that jail sentences were inappropriate for marijuana because alcohol and tobacco seemed bigger problems. Today he says, "Marijuana is a nasty drug epidemic that is the number one priority. If you would have told me in 1974 that marijuana was going to become *the* big drug problem—23 million users, 4 million under the age of eighteen and more twelve-seventeen-year-olds smoking marijuana than cigarettes—I wouldn't have believed it."[9]

According to Dr. DuPont, the notion that marijuana is harmless and its use a normal part of adolescence has been one of the most dangerous pieces of misinformation in the past two decades.

While PCP and marijuana are pleasurable, popular drugs, cocaine is the "in" drug of the '80s. It is found in the executive office, on the professional sports circuit, among television stars, and in the homes of the wealthy. The National Institute on Drug Abuse estimates that 15 million Americans have tried cocaine and that 4.5 million use it regularly. It is the most expensive illegal drug in use. Street sales in 1983 exceeded $32 billion, putting cocaine ahead of 98 percent of the Fortune 500 corporations in gross revenues! Miami is now the cocaine capital of the U.S.

What leads people to this white powder derived from the Indian's cocoa plants in the Andes mountains? Users say snorting cocaine is one of the most pleasurable experiences possible and that no serious side effects result. The euphoria produced may last up to an hour and brings unusual feelings of well-being and self-confidence.

"Cocaine is a source of transcendental joy, a liberator of creative imagination, and a sublime energizer," said one user.

For this experience, a woman restaurant operator spent $60,000 a year on her cocaine habit. Another woman spent more than $1 million during the ten years she was addicted. Cocaine led a promising stockbroker into stealthy visits to the executive washroom for new fixes. And it has driven thousands of people into burglary, embezzlement, and prostitution to support their expensive habit.

It cost Christina, a successful actress at age thirty-three, $3,000 a week to support her habit of freebasing 3 to 8 grams of coke a day. She ended up deep in debt and subject to recurring attacks of "coke bugs." And singer Sam Moore, now back on the stage again free of drugs, says he used to spend up to $400 a day for his use of heroin and cocaine.

Even higher prices are paid for the fleeting pleasures of cocaine. Strong psychic dependence can result, leading to almost continual consumption. Miami Dolphin football defensive end Don Reese said that when he used cocaine, the drug dominated his life almost every minute. "Eventually it took control of me and almost killed me," he confessed.[10]

Most cocaine users suffer severe depression after the drug wears off. Their productivity and human relationships suffer. Abuse of the drug can lead to cocaine psychosis, simulating a nervous breakdown. Even ordinary use can cause restriction of the blood vessels, ulcerations of the mucous membrane of the nose, and collapse of the septum dividing the nostrils.

"If people knew what I know about cocaine, they wouldn't go near it," says Dr. Ron Siegel, psychopharmacist and leading authority on the results of cocaine use.[11] And Dr. Charles Schuster, a physician, insists, "Cocaine abuse can cause users to become irritable, suspicious, paranoid, have hallucinations, become totally preoccupied with obtaining and using the drug, and eventually suffer a mental breakdown caused by cocaine's toxicity."[12]

That was the tragic story told by a promising university professor, Susan Clarkson, in a national journal. "Within four years, cocaine cost me my job, my husband, my self-respect, even my daughter," she confessed. "When my habit grew so that I could no longer get enough from friends, I found a part-time dealer on campus. Coke wasn't hard to find. My problem was guilt—I couldn't live with myself. One day I just exploded and walked away from everything. Officially, it was called a medical leave, but I knew that, for me, it was the end."

Eventually, Susan was arrested for possession and spent six months in prison. She is still scarred from the experience. "I can't talk about it," she says, with fear in her voice. "The only way I can go on with my life is to tell myself that the pathetic creature in that filthy place was never me."[13]

When the news broke about cocaine use by professional basketball players, "I didn't even read the stories," said a retired player
from Harlem. "The headlines might as well have said that most
players get out of bed in the morning. It's true, but it's not news."
This was his reaction to the *Los Angeles Times* report that in 1980
between 40 and 75 percent of National Basketball Association
players use cocaine—and as many as 10 percent seek the more
dangerous and intense high of freebasing. But among professional
athletes there are also some warning voices. One of them is former
Globetrotter Bobby Hunter, who declared, "I don't worry about
sounding sanctimonious. Something is either right or it's wrong.
I've been told a thousand reasons for a player using coke. And none
of them are right."[14]

A few years ago the nation's capital was shocked when it learned
of an eight-year-old Washington, D.C. boy who had become a
heroin addict. He lived with his mother, also an addict, and her
live-in lover, who had turned the home into a drug center and a
gathering place for junkies. Subsequent investigation revealed he
was not the only child addict in the city. Drugs had become a way
of life for many children. In fact, the heroin problem in Washington
has grown to what some call epidemic proportions, and Dr. Alyce
Gulatte, director of the Howard University Drug Abuse Clinic,
lamented that "heroin is destroying the city."[15]

WHY SUCH WIDE USE?

Since the mind drugs have the potential for so
much havoc, why do so many people continue to turn to them in
such large numbers? Some reasons suggested in a study of a survey
of high-school students by *Campus Life* magazine. In the words of
the students themselves:

1. "Man, there's nothing else to do."
2. "I lose all my worries and imagine many things."
3. "It blows my parents' minds."
4. "I just can't take all the tension."
5. "Me? I was just curious. That's all."
6. "I don't mind saying it. I'm just a failure."
7. "Drugs will help me realize my true potential."

8. "Drugs will help me find new religious experience and forget myself."[16]

These range all the way from boredom and despair to high idealism and reflect the complex motivations that lead people onto the drug scene. They describe many young people in our church groups as well as more sophisticated nominal members.

HOW SHOULD CHRISTIANS RESPOND?

Christians must decide how to respond to this unreal world of drug-induced euphoria or crazed hyperactivity. Although the use of natural drugs goes back to Bible times— marijuana was used more than 5,000 years ago—few specific references to drugs appear in Scripture.

However, the Bible does give universal guidelines for a Christian lifestyle that apply to the changing mores of society. These guidelines should lead a conscientious Christian to avoid using sensual drugs for merely pleasurable feelings and reserve them only for therapeutic use under a doctor's guidance. These guidelines are expressed in six biblical concepts:

1. *Obedience to civil law.* "Everyone must submit himself to the governing authorities, for there is no authority except that which God has established. The authorities that exist have been established by God. Consequently, he who rebels against the authority is rebelling against what God has instituted, and those who do so will bring judgment on themselves" (Rom. 13:1-2).

If the Apostle Paul thought a Christian should be obedient to government in a totalitarian state, we should be equally obedient in a democratic society. The inescapable conclusion from his argument that government is established by God for the orderly rule of people is that Christian obedience to law is honoring to God. When laws make drug usage a crime, the Christian has no choice— he must forego recreational drugs.

2. *Stewardship of the body.* "Do you not know that your body is a temple of the Holy Spirit, who is in you, whom you have received from God? You are not your own; you were bought at a price. Therefore honor God with your body" (1 Cor. 6:19-20).

Christianity is unique among religions of the world in its emphasis upon the human body. So important is the body in biblical
revelation that it is destined to live forever. The Christian doctrine
of immortality refers to the body as well as the soul. If Adam and
Eve had not sinned in the Garden, where they had continual access
to the tree of life, they would have lived forever in Paradise in their
physical bodies.

When Christ rose from the dead on the first Easter, His body was
the firstfruit of the ultimate physical resurrection of all God's
children. The resurrection body differs from the original body. But
enough individuating dust of our old bodies will be re-created to
give us eternal identity through them. Of course, resurrection is a
mystery and a miracle but no greater than the miracle of Creation
in the first place. If we believe one, we can believe the other.

Having entrusted to us in this life a body with an eternal dimension, God has chosen to fill it with His own presence through the
Holy Spirit. Like the holy of holies in the Old Testament tabernacle,
lighted by the Shekinah glory of God's presence, our bodies are
indwelt by God as His temples in the world today.

The Old Testament is filled with precautions about caring for the
temple on Mt. Zion in ways that are appropriate for a holy God.
The New Testament is filled with guidance on how we today are to
be temple-keepers through the care and use of our bodies.

Daniel's Abomination of Desolation in the temple probably referred to invaders who ransacked the temple in Jerusalem, spilling
the blood of unclean animals on the sacred furniture. That abomination is repeated in the human temples of the Holy Spirit when
we deliberately defile our bodies with sensual drugs.

Paul lamented that the Romans degraded their bodies with one
another (Rom. 1:24). He might well lament the prostitution of
bodies today in the drug cult.

How well I remember a young man of the Rastafarian cult who,
after a service in the Virgin Islands, committed his life to Christ.
When I returned a year later, he was still in the church. But his new
Christian friends concluded sadly that his years of drug abuse had
left him with irreparable brain damage, limiting him the rest of his
life. The temple had been damaged.

We are to be good stewards of our bodies for the glory of God.

Christian stewardship is even broader and includes the constructive use of our time and money as well as our bodies, all of which can be wasted through drugs.

3. *The living sacrifice of the body*: "Therefore, I urge you brothers, in view of God's mercy, to offer your bodies as living sacrifices, holy and pleasing to God—which is your spiritual worship" (Rom. 12:1).

The non-Christian world often has sacrificed human bodies to pagan gods. People have been burned on altars, thrown into rivers, or fed to animals. Christ, however, calls for our bodies to be living sacrifices—dead but alive. Ideally, our bodies are to be dead to selfish exploitation and alive to God and His purposes.

When we yield ourselves to Christ, we yield Him our bodies as well as our souls. The two, in fact, are inseparable and simply constitute two dimensions of a single existence.

How can we offer our bodies to God? We can begin with the five senses of physical awareness: tasting, smelling, seeing, hearing, and feeling. One by one, we can dedicate to God our tongues, noses, eyes, ears, and hands. They are the body organs which keep us in contact with our world. They respond to the multibillion dollar trade in stimulants, narcotics, depressants, hallucinogens, and synthetic/refined chemicals of our time.

We can offer the organs of our bodies to God in a continuing act of worship so that: our tongues will not taste marijuana or liquor; our noses will not inhale cocaine or angel dust; our eyes will not seek out drug pushers; our ears will not listen to siren calls of communal addicts; and our hands will not touch the pills, leaves, powder, pipes, or syringes that characterize this contemporary misuse of the human body.

4. *The fullness of the Spirit*: "Do not get drunk on wine, which leads to debauchery. Instead, be filled with the Spirit. Speak to one another with psalms, hymns, and spiritual songs. Sing and make music in your heart to the Lord" (Eph. 5:18).

Alcohol is one sensual drug for which Paul recommends an antidote: instead of being filled with wine and becoming drunk, be filled with the Spirit and become joyful. The spiritual songs of the believer contrast with the drunken songs of the alcoholic and the shrieks of the LSD paranoic.

The Holy Spirit is alive in such diverse and unusual ways in the world today that being filled with Him is the beginning of an exciting adventure. Instead of the euphoria caused by drugs, Christians experience the peace, joy, and contentment of the Spirit described in Philippians 4. In Christ a spiritual euphoria exists that is based on reality, has no hangovers, and makes us fun to live with. People who search for personal victory over problems or for inner transcendental experience—both of which lead so many to drugs—can find fulfillment in the Holy Spirit.

How can one be filled with the Spirit? Can a Christian have more of Him than he already has? No. If he is a Christian, he already has all there is of the Holy Spirit. One can't have just part of the Holy Spirit. He has none or all of Him. But as G. Arvid Gordh, a godly teacher of mine, used to say years ago, "The big question is not, 'Do I have all of the Holy Spirit?' but—'Does the Holy Spirit have all of me?' " While it is not possible for us to have more of the Holy Spirit it is possible for the Holy Spirit to have more of us.

Being spirit-controlled calls for daily obedience to Him. Peter declared after Pentecost that the Holy Spirit is given to those who obey Him (Acts 5:32). The old chorus asking, "Spirit of the living God fall afresh on me," could better be sung, "Spirit of the living God take control of me." Instead of drugs controlling the brain center, the Spirit can control the *will* center of the Christian. As He does so, He leads the believer into the pleasurable experience of His fullness.

5. *The lordship of Christ*: "But in your hearts set apart Christ as Lord...(1 Peter 3:15). I have never forgotten one of the profound impressions made upon me when I was a high school student. I had been reading the daily devotional book *Abundant Living* by Dr. E. Stanley Jones on the disciplined life under the lordship of Christ. One of Dr. Jones' essays began with a reference to his friends who smoked.

"It would have been easier to have left out this section," he wrote, "but the future of the world is in the hands of disciplined people. The user of tobacco is undisciplined."[17] It is a contradiction to call Christ Master if at times nicotine is master, and we must respond to its call.

When Dr. Jones wrote this, we were just beginning to learn

about the physical problems caused by smoking. But simply because I wanted Christ to be the only Lord in my life, I resolved then not to join my teenage friends in using tobacco. I have been glad to this day for that decision.

The Apostle Paul has a definitive statement about addictive practices: " 'Everything is permissible for me—but I will not be mastered by anything' " (1 Cor. 6:12). However legal a practice may be—as tobacco and alcohol are in our time—we would do well to say with Paul, "I will not be a slave to anything. I am a love slave of Christ alone."

If this principle is true for lawful practices, how much more must it be true for illegal ones such as sensual drugs?

6. *Strength in Christ to overcome life's problems*: "I have learned to be content whatever the circumstances. I know what it is to be in need, and I know what it is to have plenty. I have learned the secret of being content in any and every situation, whether well fed or hungry, whether living in plenty or in want. I can do everything through Him who gives me strength" (Phil. 4:11-13).

Thousands of people turn to drugs to cope with their problems. Cocaine, for example, often is in the professional world because it gives a quick, fleeting sense of self-confidence for someone who must participate in a television show, perform in a movie, or take part in an interview or board meeting.

Heroin, often cocaine's counterpart, provides a soothing escape from reality so that a person can function as though problems didn't exist. Many people "mainline" both cocaine and heroin into their veins simultaneously, for a double feeling of alertness and relaxation as they confront the tensions of their lives.

For such people, Paul's witness to the Philippians is very relevant. When he talks about discovering contentment in all circumstances, he uses a Greek word for contentment which has been transliterated into English as ataractic. A word used mostly by physicians, it means "tranquilizer." Not in drugs, but in Christ Paul found tranquility. When he wrote these words, he had been in prison four years and had just been unjustly condemned to death!

In its original compound expressions, *ataractic* means to be independent of circumstances. The sun may be shining or a storm may be howling. It's all right. Christ is our strength. Imprisoned or

free, we have Christ. Forsaken or surrounded, we can depend on
Christ. Our ultimate independence from the changing circumstances of life is in Him.

When this is true, we can also say with Paul, "For to me, to live is
Christ and to die is gain" (Phil. 1:21). To live or die. It's all right
either way when Christ is the strength by our side. Christ gives an
enduring contentment, not one that fades in an hour or is followed
by depression and, perhaps, suicide.

These six biblical concepts bear on the use of sensual drugs by
Christians: (1) obedience to civil law; (2) stewardship of the body;
(3) the living sacrifice of the body; (4) fullness of the Holy Spirit;
(5) the lordship of Christ, and (6) the strength in Christ to
overcome life's problems.

These reinforce the warnings of the medical world and provide
biblical insight into an alternative Christian lifestyle for all people.
Christ provides the benefits sought in drugs without the problems
which accompany them—and He provides much more!

FOUR

THE GAMBLING MANIA

"We're gamblers, so you'll find us in the casinos about 90 percent of the time," Ellen McGee said to her friends who were celebrating her seventieth birthday just before she took off again from Minneapolis for Las Vegas, Nevada.

Together with a friend, she and her husband make up a trio of high-flying Minnesotans who have an ongoing love affair with the gambling capital of America. During the past six years, the McGees and their friend have flown there forty times on chartered flights—so many times, in fact, that their travel agency feted them as its most frequent fliers to Las Vegas. The three of them received gifts of round-trip flights there and were publicized in the agency's magazine. "Actually," said their friend, "we go to Las Vegas an average of once a month."[1] For this trio, gambling has become their regular recreation.

In contrast, in 1983 the sports world was stunned when Art Schlicter, rookie quarterback for the Baltimore Colts football team, confessed to police that he had lost $389,000 betting with Baltimore bookmakers.[2] The former Ohio State All-American was banned from the National Football League as punishment. After a year out of football, he came back, professing that gambling was a thing of the past in his life.

Most adult Americans can be found somewhere between the

50

extremes of fun and compulsion in gambling. An estimated two-thirds of them place some kind of bet regularly. This ratio is even worse in England where 80 percent of all adults gamble. It is a growing problem for the Christian church because its members are being drawn into it innocently, seriously, or compulsively as a result of peer pressure.

A NATION OF GAMBLERS

Our entire nation seems to be on a gambling spree. In 1983, according to Public Gaming Research of Maryland, legal gambling totaled $24 billion and illegal bets probably exceeded an additional $32 billion. Thus, a total stake of at least $56 billion changed hands through gambling. Consultant and author John Scarne, after conducting a survey of 100,000 gamblers, places the figure much higher and pegs the volume of bets as high as one-third of our gross national product. He puts the annual total somewhere between $500 billion and $1 trillion![3]

Atlantic City is second only to Las Vegas in gambling. In 1982 alone, 27 million visitors went there to gamble. The gross winnings of the nine casinos exceeded $1.5 billion before expenses and taxes. Incidentally, per capita crime has tripled in Atlantic City since the advent of legalized gambling. Its parent state of New Jersey now raises 7 percent of its annual budget through taxes on gambling. It is noteworthy that the *New York Times* observed that to support government by such gambling is economic immorality.

Every year in the last three decades more people have paid their way to horse racing tracks than to any of the popular team sports. This is not because they love animals or want to spend an afternoon in the sun. They simply want to make one quick, big killing. And, though 90 percent of all gamblers lose, they hope to beat the odds.

Ironically, in some instances gambling is abetted by certain churches that seek to raise funds through their distinctive game of chance—Bingo—and rely on this method more heavily than on the voluntary tithes and offerings of their members. Virgil Peterson, operating director of the Chicago Crime Commission, commented wryly about this, saying that "churches now run illegal gambling games because that's a sure way of getting money for holy causes from people who otherwise wouldn't contribute if the Almighty pushed a .45 at them." Surveys have found that an estimated 44 percent of the people living in the states where Bingo is illegal think it is legal because of its close association with churches and charitable groups. All of this means that Christians ought to acquaint themselves with the issue of gambling and, hopefully, be ready to resist the pressures of their culture to endorse it. Such acquaintanceship can come from looking at a few basic questions.

WHAT IS GAMBLING?

Joan Halliday and Peter Fuller, writing in the *Psychology of Gambling*, succinctly defined gambling as "a reallocation of wealth, on the basis of deliberate risk, involving gain to one party and loss to another, usually without the introduction of productive work on either side. The determining process always involves an element of chance and may be only by chance."[4]

Gambling can be distinguished from other forms of risk-taking by three elements which must coexist: (1) a *payment* is involved, for (2) a *prize* to be awarded, on the (3) basis of *chance*, sometimes accompanied by skill.

When any one of these three elements is missing, there may be pseudogambling—gaining money without performance or service—but not bona fide gambling. All of life is characterized by risk-taking, such as making financial investments, beginning business ventures, or establishing insurance hedges. Yet these risks are different from gambling in that productive work is involved, empirical data is used as a basis for decision-making, and adverse experiences often can be offset through wise management.

Nevertheless, the prevalence of risk in so many legitimate personal and professional endeavors may be partially responsible for America's toleration of gambling risks.

Gambling, it may be concluded, is the distribution of money by chance, instead of by need or services rendered or expected.

WHY DO PEOPLE GAMBLE?

There are several motivations that keep the wheel of chance spinning for Americans. The basic ones:

1. *Poverty*. So many people live near or below the poverty line

in the U.S. that the possibility of making large amounts of money from a small investment is enticing. Gambling is regressive in that it appeals so powerfully to the poor who can't afford to risk their money that way but who do so out of frustration over their economic needs.

2. *Greed.* People at all financial levels are motivated by greed—the insatiable desire for more. It was called avarice by medieval Christians and listed as one of the seven deadly sins. When comedian Red Skelton was performing in England, he was asked why he continued to make appearances though retired. He answered facetiously, "Because I'm addicted to money." Often this is a way of life for gamblers. One forty-one-year-old store owner, commenting on the sixteen years he was on the gambling merry-go-round, said, "I'd close my eyes and see myself winning huge sums of money, hobnobbing with the beautiful people, driving a luxury car. I was the guy who made the casino close the table because I cleaned them out."[5]

3. *Entertainment.* The legitimate desire for fun and escape lead many to the gambling tables. It is but a small step from playing a game of cards for fun to placing a wager on the outcome. And then it's a somewhat larger step when one joins the professional gamesters to pit his luck—and fortune—against theirs. Much of it is associated with luxurious surroundings, colored lights, music, and erotic entertainment. Houses of prostitution flourish in gambling centers.

4. *Excitement.* The possibility of winning huge sums and the suspense involved in the action makes the adrenalin flow faster and provides a thrill for the gambler. Many gamblers insist that this is their chief drive.

5. *Compulsion.* Robert Custer, a Veterans Administration psychiatrist, spoke of compulsive gambling in these terms: "[It] is strikingly similar to a drug habit [and] probably one of the purest forms of psychological addiction known. Compulsive gamblers are stimulated by gambling, get high on it, and have withdrawal symptoms when they stop."[6]

To all of these motivations must be added what Mann and Bock call the decline of moral values and the work ethic in America. They write: "Gambling's get-rich-quick appeal appears to mock capitalism's core values—disciplined work habits, thrift, prudence, adherence to routine, and the relationship between effort and reward."[7] As a result, Americans are turning to gambling in increasing numbers and are seeking to legalize it in many states.

WHAT OPTIONS ARE THERE
FOR GAMBLING?

When David McKenna, now president of Asbury Theological Seminary, was chairman of the governor's ad hoc committee on gambling for the state of Washington, he identified three basic arenas of gambling: social, professional, and governmental. Social gambling refers simply to a group of friends involved in games of chance as amateurs. Estimates indicate that one-third of the nation may violate the law by playing cards for money or by wagering pools of money on sports events. No professionals are involved. In most instances the laws are neither enforced nor enforceable.

Professional gambling involves a professional operator, a network of assistants, and a payoff system to reward them out of the proceeds. Governmental gambling includes such games of chance as lotteries and pari-mutuel betting to raise money for the public treasury in lieu of additional taxes.

Gambling may be further defined by four basic types described by Halliday and Fuller in their significant treatise on gambling:[8]

□ *Gaming*—an exchange of money in which chance plays a part (such as roulette)

□ *Betting*—staking money on a future event, the outcome is doubtful or unknown to the participants (such as horse racing)

□ *Lotteries*—distribution of a mutually contributed pool of money by lot (such as football pools)

□ *Speculation*—the gambling aspects of the commodities market (such as commodities speculation)

The first three types provide a bewildering number of options for the gambler looking for a sure thing. A checkered pattern exists in America for him because different states have legalized different games of chance. Only four states do not permit any legalized gambling. For those who want to gamble legally, at least nine options exist somewhere in the United States:

1. *Bingo* (legalized in forty-three states). While Bingo has been stereotyped as a woman's game, it actually is popular with men as well. The stakes are low, averaging $6 a night. But in 1975 more was wagered on Bingo than in all Nevada casinos that year. The takeout rate—amount won—is about 33 percent. In Minnesota where Bingo is illegal, Indian tribes have set up huge Bingo parlors on their autonomous reservations and attract full houses regularly.

2. *Horse Racing* (legalized in thirty-three states). In 1980, gamblers bet $11.2 billion on horses with a takeout of 15 to 18 percent, including 5 percent to the state where the betting occurred. Parimutuel betting—where participants bet against each other rather than against the broker—is continuing to be legalized by states. About 85 percent of the bets are returned in payoffs on the first three horses—win, place, and show. As many as 15 percent of all adults engage in gambling on horses.

3. *Lotteries* (legalized in eighteen states up to 1984 and in additional ones since). About 50 million people purchase lottery tickets. Legalized only since 1964, lotteries now outdraw most other forms of legal betting. In 1979, hopeful gamblers spent $1.8 billion on lottery tickets. Because tickets are cheap, lotteries appeal to millions of poor people, causing them to risk money they can't afford to lose. What's more, the odds are heavily stacked against them.

4. *Numbers* (legalized in sixteen states). Tickets are purchased and winners' numbers are drawn similar to the lottery. The game differs in the way winning combinations of numbers are selected. It is just as exploitive. In New York City alone, an estimated 100,000 people play the numbers daily, operators getting 60 percent of the take.

Twenty-five percent goes to the runners (people who transmit the tickets). An average numbers racket man earns up to $60,000 a year. Nevertheless, because the numbers game is low-cost and easily accessible, two-thirds of inner-city adults take this gambling risk.

5. *Dog Racing* (legalized in fourteen states). Since introduced in South Dakota in 1904, dog racing has grown in popularity. It now involves 4 percent of the gambling population with a cumulative stake of $2 billion.

6. *Jai alai* (legalized in five states). Of the five states sponsoring *jai-alai* betting—a game similar to handball but with wicker baskets on the arms—Florida leads. In 1983, 6.5 million people spent $500 million on this form of gambling.

7. *Sports* (legalized in four states). Betting on professional and amateur sports has not been legitimized to the same extent as other forms of gambling. As a result, sports betting constitutes the greatest form of illegal gambling in the U.S.

8. *Off-track betting* (legalized in four states). This allows a person to gamble on horses without being at the track.

9. *Casinos* (legalized in three states). Nevada and New Jersey are vying to become the gambling capital of the nation. New Jersey now is in the lead because of the proximity of 16 million potential gamblers to Atlantic City's boardwalk. In Nevada in a recent year, $3.6 billion was tallied, with $169.7 million going for state taxes. Nevada has 67,000 slot machines, many in restrooms and at departing gates at airports. Some casinos pay airfare, lodging, and food costs of their patrons to have a chance at their money.

More than three-fourths of all Americans favor legalized gambling, and many are lobbying in the states to open additional doors. The major arguments being advanced for legalizing gambling are that it will provide revenue for state treasuries, that gambling can better be controlled, that legalization will reduce criminal exploitation, and that legal games of chance will channel a human impulse too powerful to be eliminated by law. These are all plausible reasons and led even the distinguished director of one of America's Crime Investigating Committees to publicly declare himself in favor of legalizing gambling.

It seems to me, however, that the social price paid for gambling is so great that Americans no longer can afford it. Christians should oppose the present surge of legalization and call for stricter enforcement of existing laws against gambling.

WHAT IS THE SOCIAL PRICE OF GAMBLING?

Perhaps the most serious price of social gambling is in terms of human dignity when a person becomes addicted to *compulsive gambling*. This fate has befallen up to 10 million gamblers in the United States, according to an estimate made in 1980 by the National Council on Compulsive Gambling.[9] This suggests that already there may be as many compulsive gamblers in our nation as there are alcoholics.

It is not surprising, therefore, that a self-help organization exists for them also, Gamblers Anonymous. This group defines compulsive gambling as an "illness, progressive in nature, which can never be cured but can be arrested." Symptoms of this illness include his readiness to take chances habitually, his allowing the game to preclude all other interests, his continuous optimism and inability to learn from defeat, his refusal to stop when winning, his risking of too much, and his anticipation of the pleasure—pain tension during the game.

Compulsive gambling, according to Dr. Robert Politzer, director of the John Hopkins Compulsive Gambling Center, is "an impulsive disorder that can be classified with kleptomania and pyromania."[10] It is sobering that in 1980 the American Psychiatric Association certified pathological gambling as a mental disorder. The gambler's mood successively moves from an initial feeling of immunity against the odds, to a feeling of being betrayed over subsequent losses, to a deep compulsion to get even by winning back, to the employment of illegal methods—embezzlement, credit cards, bad checks—to continue gambling, and ultimately to a sense of despair and bottoming out. Chronic gamblers play for high emotional stakes.

In terms of human damage, compulsive gambling can be extremely destructive. Politzer estimates that each compulsive gambler disrupts the lives of ten to seventeen other people, including relatives, co-workers, and creditors. The economic cost also is high. The average compulsive gambler usually bets twice what he makes and costs society approximately $40,000 a year.[11]

The gambling compulsion has infected the high-school crowd with nearly 2 percent of the students in one survey showing outward signs of already being compulsive gamblers. Eighty-six percent of 900 students reported that they had gambled within the past year, half of them illegally in casinos closed to minors. The disease of gambling is infectious and knows no age limits.

Another social price of gambling is to be seen in the *organized crime* that it spawns, a loose federation of the Mafia-type groups in control of most illegal gambling in the United States. John Winters, an investigative reporter with the *Arizona Republic,* defines organized crime as "a continuing conspiracy to accumulate wealth in defiance of the law."[12]

Illegal gambling has become one of the safest ways for organized crime to make big money and is its greatest source of revenue. Like other forms of organized criminal activity, illegal gambling supplies illicit goods or services, guarantees profits through monopolistic or oligarchic competition, and employs fear and violence to maintain control of the market. As a result, organized crime controls 75 percent of all illegal gambling. Many of the nearly 500,000 career criminals in the U.S. are involved in illegal gambling.

Society also is injured by other crimes financed by gambling proceeds, such as traffic in drugs and penetration of legal businesses as fronts. The criminal effects of gambling are so widespread that many police officers and courts do not take them seriously and lawbreakers escape punishment. Respect for the law is thereby diminished.

Concomitant with the criminal aspect of gambling is the price paid in the *corruption of public officials.* This includes police officers, judges, legislators, and commission members. All are subject to bribery, and regularly some weak official capitulates. When a race track was proposed for Tulsa, Oklahoma, the *Tulsa World* reported that a key promoter requested $2.4 million to be paid in order to influence the racing commission. The commission had previously turned down the application of Green County Racing, Inc. for a track estimated to cost in excess of $100 million. One person was arrested and charged with extortion in connection with this attempt to influence the commission.[13]

Estes Kefauver, at one time chairman of a Congressional Crime Committee, reported that in his investigations he discovered in one city that the original bankroll of a quarter of a million dollars for one illegal operation was made in an armored car in which the sheriff owned an interest. The armored car also picked up the proceeds of the illegal gambling operation every day. The guards on the armored car, as well as the guards at the gambling casino, were furnished by the sheriff. Kefauver also reported that in another city the sheriff's brother was operating an illegal lottery in the jail!

In his book *New Complete Guide to Gambling*, John Scarne extends this kind of collusion by writing, "No other form of illegal gambling... enjoys such effective police and political protection as illegal bookmaking."[14]

Another serious price of gambling is, again, its *exploitation of the poor*. While people of all income brackets gamble, there is ample evidence that a higher percentage of poor people's income is lost in this way. Out of desperation, they reach for possible help only to be driven deeper into poverty and despair. They are the majority participants in the numbers racket and in state operated lotteries. The publicity given to astronomical lottery winnings in 1984—$20 million in New York and $40 million in Illinois—mask the odds of 13 million to 1 for winning. A critical article in the July 1983 *Harpers* magazine stated that, statistically, death by lightning is seven times more likely than winning $1 million in a typical game in which 20 million $1 tickets are sold.

The poor are involved at the casinos also. A recent scholarly probe into the situation in Atlantic City concluded that "every study of casino gambling has indicated its regressive nature, that is, that lower income groups spent a greater percentage of their income on gambling than other income groups."[15]

There are other serious social prices to be paid for gambling, such as the scandal of cheating at the games and white-collar crime committed to make up for gambling losses. All establish a strong case for making our decision about gambling on a moral basis. The morality of gambling was summarized by Larry Braidfast of the Southern Baptist Christian Life Commission in his statement: "An industry which wrecks lives, leads to an increased crime rate, fails to deliver what it promises in financial rewards, breaks homes, leaves families in financial stress, and preys upon the poor is not an industry which is a matter of personality."[16]

WHAT THEOLOGICAL CONCERNS EXIST?

For the Christian there are serious theological concerns, because gambling contradicts some basic biblical assumptions. However, not all Christians interpret the Bible the same on these points. Traditionally, the Roman Catholic church has taken a more lenient stance toward gambling by incorporating Bingo games into its fund-raising programs.

Cardinal Cushing once commented to the Boston police: "In my theology, gambling itself is not a sin any more than taking a glass of beer or hard liquor is a sin."[17]

Official Protestant positions have followed a harder line on gambling. But, to be sure, significant exceptions exist on both sides. In my judgment, gambling violates five fundamental theological concepts, which should cause Christians to seriously question the practice:

1. *God's universe is one of order and not chance.* Dr. Arthur Holmes, professor of philosophy at Wheaton College, contrasts the gambler's world view with the biblical world view. The gambler's world is ruled by artificially created chance, devoid of clearly predictable outcomes, unsusceptible to meaningful planning and lacking in productive energy.[18] In God's providence, the world operates consistently by laws that He has established and moves toward the systematic fulfillment of His master plan. Chance as a way of life is incongruous in such a universe.

Long ago, Archbishop of Canterbury William Temple declared that the glorification of mere chance is indeed a denial of the divine order of nature. An old Methodist declaration on gambling states: "The resort to gambling is a virtual denial of faith in God and an ordered universe, putting in its place an appeal to blind chance, prompted neither by love nor rectitude."[19]

Isaiah rebuked people who forsake the Lord to "spread a table for Fortune and fill bowls of mixed wine for Destiny" (Isa. 65:11-12).

2. *Advancement in life is based upon work.* From the time the first family was expulsed from the Garden of Eden, to this day, work has been ordained by God for advancement in life. The Old Testament relfects this: "By the sweat of your brow you will eat your food" (Gen. 3:19); as does the New Testament: " 'If a man will not work, he shall not eat' " (2 Thes. 3:10).

Both precepts, by maximizing the role of work in life, minimize nonproductive activity such as gambling as a valid way of advancement. The Protestant work ethic is being strained in America these days, but it still exists as an ideal for many.

3. *Money is a trust to be handled wisely.* This certainly is the clear teaching of Jesus' Parable of the Talents (Matt. 25:14-30). Money here is viewed as a responsibility for which Christians are accountable. This teaching could be included in Paul's declaration: "Now it is required that those who have been given a trust must prove faithful" (1 Cor. 4:2).

In this broad view, not only a tithe—10 percent—belongs to God, but 100 percent of one's income. All of our resources simply have been entrusted to us to expend on God's behalf.

We have no more ultimate right over the 90 percent than over the 10 percent. We are to invest it all to the glory of God. As long ago as 1937, while he was still Archbishop of York, Temple insisted that the Christian who risks money haphazardly disregards the church's insistence that material possessions are a trust from God. We must account to Him for our use of them.

Such a concept leaves no place for careless stewardship or for the deliberate courting of the loss of all. Gambling thus is antithetical to Christian stewardship because it is a waste of both time and treasure, two of a person's most valuable assets.

4. *Covetousness is to be avoided.* Our Saviour's warning, "Watch out! Be on your guard against all kinds of greed" (Luke 12:15) certainly must include gambling. Gambling grows out of greed and fosters covetousness. To this can be added the Apostle Paul's sober observation: "For the love of money is a root of all kinds of evil. Some people, eager for money, have wandered from the faith and pierced themselves with many griefs" (1 Tim. 6:10).

Some people believe that the tenth commandment—the tenth "Lifeline," as Edith Schaeffer calls it—is the key commandment: "Thou shalt not covet" (Deut. 5:21, KJV).[20] Covetousness is the source for breaking most of the commandments. The persistent appeal of gambling to the covetous, grasping spirit is in opposition to all Jesus taught about the unselfish, giving spirit.

One gambling addict confessed in a *U.S. News and World Report* article, "You never really come out ahead in gambling. Even when you win, you still lose because you always want to parlay the money into a bigger win—and then you lose it all." Big gamblers usually die poor. The odds are too great.

The covetous spirit never can be satisfied. Covetousness makes a god of mammon and leads to materialism as a way of life. The avaricious quest for money by chance has no place in the life of a Christian who is trusting God to supply his needs.

5. *Neighbors are to be loved unselfishly.* The second commandment (Luke 10:27) according to Christ, is "Love your neighbor as yourself" (Matt. 22:39). This verse is a more positive rendering of the Golden Rule: "In everything, do to others what you would have them do to you" (Matt. 7:12). We are our brother's keeper. We cannot knowingly inflict on our brother the pain and degradation which accompanies gambling. If I win, he loses, and in the process we both lose.

Gambling manipulates people for personal profit. It is unworthy of the followers of Christ. Virgil Peterson, of the Chicago Crime Commission, observed: "Gambling is always based on a desire to get something for nothing, to take something away from someone else while giving nothing in return."

These five biblical concepts undercut a valid place for gambling in the life of a Christian. To be sure, they are broad biblical teachings applied to a specific problem. Apart from Isaiah 65:11-12, the Bible has no direct references to gambling as we know it. While casting lots to ascertain God's will was common before the coming of the Holy Spirit at Pentecost—including priests using the stones Urim and Tummin from their breastplates—this was not gambling. There was no exchange of money and no personal gain for one person and loss for another.

Casting lots was a pre-Christian search for divine direction. Today we find God's will through the Holy Spirit and His Word. Even when soldiers cast lots at the cross to parcel out Christ's clothing while He was dying for them—however reprehensible—at the most it was pseudogambling. Yet, the Bible does give a coherent theological world view to help us focus on gambling. Our five biblical concepts about creation, work, money, contentment, and our neighbor stand in opposition to gambling.

George Washington once aptly described gambling: "It is the child of avarice, the brother of iniquity, and the father of mischief." America is afflicted with a gambling mania. It is not the first time in our history we've experienced this problem, nor are we the only nation affected. The times do not call for a new generation of bluenoses—people who try to impose their moral views on others—or professional do-gooders. What is needed are Christians who set a voluntary example of personal self-discipline and thereby help turn the tide against gambling.

All of us can join in J. Clark Gibson's prayer, written thirty years ago, about the misuse of money through gambling:

Almighty God, who dost require of all men that they should be faithful stewards of Thy manifold gifts, we beseech Thee that in getting and spending we may not misuse our stewardship.

Deliver us from the selfishness that seeks gain without labor, or excitement without care for its cost to others. Set free those who are possessed by the gambling spirit and break the power of those who exploit their weakness.

Prosper the efforts of all who are striving to remove the evils of betting and gambling and lead all men to seek in Thee their true joy and to find in Thy service the fullness of life, through Jesus Christ our Lord. Amen.[21]

FIVE

GREED FOR MONEY

"Can I help you with your investment program?" It seemed incongruous to hear a pastor friend asking this question on the phone not long ago. When I expressed surprise, he said he had left the ministry to become an investment counselor. Though I had known him as a pastor of one of the wealthiest churches in our area, he felt he wasn't making enough money for the needs of his growing family—college tuition and all that. His solution was to leave his church for a better-paying position. Now here he was offering his services as a stockbroker.

While I mused over the shift in God's call for my friend's leadership in the church, I thought of many other friends. In these times of economic pressures, they have made similar changes. Today, instead of preaching the Gospel, they are selling insurance, real estate, gems, tours of the Holy Land, and stocks and bonds. I do not criticize them. I know that in Bible times God called persons into His service for single missions and limited terms. But I wonder about what seems a mass defection from the pulpit. It is a sober reminder to keep my own priorities as I seek God's call at successive stages in my life. I remember too well a veteran minister's sage observation that our besetting sin changes with the seasons of life. "In youth, it is sex; in middle-age, it is ambition; and in old age, it is money," he said.

Each of these probably overlaps other age-periods. This is particularly true of money. It is little wonder that early church fathers considered avarice one of the deadly sins. Jesus Himself emphasized, "You cannot serve both God and Money" (Matt. 6:24).

JESUS' CALL TO DISCIPLESHIP

Perhaps the most sobering call to discipleship is Jesus' summons in Luke 14. Here He lists the costs first in terms of personal relationships (14:26), second in personal ambitions (14:27), and third in personal possessions (14:33). He insists that we cannot be His disciples without the paying of these costs.

Then, making two military allusions, He warns us to count the cost of enlistment in His cause: consider the man who builds a sentry tower without enough money to complete it and the general who begins a battle without enough soldiers.

Often we learn that cost long after we have committed ourselves to Christ. It is particularly true of those converted to Christ in youth that the significance of discipleship shows up later when we know our vocation, our spouse, our closest friends, and what temptations are most enticing. It is then that we can affirm most meaningfully, "Yes, Lord, I still mean it. I want to follow You at any cost and be Your disciple."

The third call of Jesus—the cost in personal possessions—stands out in sharp contrast to our affluent and self-indulgent Western world: "Any of you who does not give up everything he has cannot be My disciple" (Luke 14:33). That hardly sounds American! Our emphasis is not upon net loss, but net gain—regular increases in salary, more material assets, advancement in position and compensation, enlarged fringe benefits and perquisites, and an annual increase in net personal worth. In a growth-oriented American economy, anything less than *more* is failure. How then do we apply Jesus' call to our lives? There are two aspects to be considered: the dilemma and the resolution.

THE DILEMMA

Renouncing material things—which Jesus calls His disciples to do—is foreign to our culture. The hippies of the '60s and '70s got by with little while they lived for their nonmaterial goals. They seemed a bizarre generation—bewhiskered, poorly clad, carrying all their possessions in knapsacks, and living as nomads off the land.

Their incense, strange music, and drug-induced fantasy world turned many of us off as much as it turned them on. They did not make self-renunciation an attractive ideal. They eventually turned from that lifestyle themselves. Today most are active participants in the free enterprise system and climbing the corporate ladder they once repudiated.

Their successors—a new generation of college students—want their share of worldly goods, not unworldly ideals. They've set their sights on jobs that pay well with a minimum of effort, upon country estates, two boats at every vacation dock, and plenty of leisure time. The old Puritan work *ethic* indeed has given way to the Greek pleasure ethic. Here then is our dilemma.

The early Romans said that the acquisition of material things was like drinking salt water. The more you drank the thirstier you became. The Cracker Jack slogan of our time, "The more you eat, the more you want," describes the dilemma of our Western culture. Material things—property stocks, bonds, bank accounts, gems—never satisfy. We never have enough.

Greed is simply an insatiable desire for more. To the medieval Christians, avarice was simply another way of spelling greed. To them, avarice was a human vulnerability that provided an entry point for Satan. It becomes cancerous and our very growth chokes us. Greed infects many facets of life, but it can be seen most clearly in our attitude toward material goods. For most of us, the road to riches is like an escalator going up and up. We are caught in an inescapable momentum. When is enough? One house with the mortgage paid off? Two houses, including a lake cabin? Three houses with a winter hideaway? Four houses, with a spot in Switzerland? Five houses? If we are making plenty of money, when have we spent enough on ourselves and can say, "No more"? When do we get off the escalator?

Even the richest man in the world, multibillionaire J. Paul Getty, was still using his vast sums right up to his death to make more money. Money can be leveraged, and if we give it away, we lose that power. So we are caught up in an unrelenting cycle. We then

practice what J. Oswald Sanders termed "extra corpus benevo-
lence." We keep on reinvesting money we'll never need so that it
becomes more and more. Then at our death someone else has all
the joy of giving it away or of creating new cultural attractions,
much as in the case of the J. Paul Getty Art Museum in California
that Getty himself never saw.

All of us are on this economic escalator. The GNP (gross national
product) becomes GPP (gross personal product). We must show
an increase in our net worth each year if we are to maintain our
self-respect. Who even wants to get off this escalator? Who says,
"This is enough. I don't want anymore"?

John Wesley did. Two hundred years ago in England he was
earning thirty pounds a year. He lived on twenty-eight and gave
two away. When his income doubled to sixty pounds, he still lived
on twenty-eight and gave away thirty-two. When it tripled, he
continued to live on twenty-eight giving the rest away. And when it
reached 120 pounds, he was still living on twenty-eight! Not many
of us choose to be like that.

In our own time, Catholic priest and novelist Andrew Greeley
declared, "I never wanted to be a millionaire," when he used
$850,000 in profits from his books to fund a chair at the University
of Chicago. Then he began searching for other ways to put his
money to work in worthy causes. Some people lose their multimil-
lionaire status inadvertently by bad investments in stocks. Others
lose it deliberately by good investments in people and causes.

These are the exceptions. Highly paid Madison Avenue professionals feed greed constantly by bombarding us with enticing and
sometimes subliminal demonstrations of why we absolutely must
have certain products. Until then we never even knew the need
existed. No matter that there may be a built-in obsolescence to
some products or that others may quickly go out of style. Or that
we may not be able to afford them. Our neighbors are buying and
we need them now.

Greed is whetted, in part, by a credit card society in which
people buy now and *really* pay later. Our greed also is fueled by
superstar salaries that have no relationship to productivity or to a
logical national salary framework—professional athletes, movie
stars, or television performers. A $4 million contract signed by a

baseball player makes our ordinary salary seem paltry. We feel cheated and want more. Greed also is fueled by the lotteries increasingly being legalized state by state. Even though the odds may be 1,000 to 1 against the gambler, someone, in fact, does win. That largest lottery prize to date—$40 million in Illinois—creates in most of us a desire to achieve riches some easy way. Yet the Illinois winner found out the hard way that money can also create huge problems!

In our increasingly litigious society, greed also is fanned by the large multimillion dollar court settlements for personal damages. Often the awards are so great that a person could not spend them in a lifetime. Additional punitive awards are frequently assessed against corporations, and the costs are passed on to consumers in increased prices so that they alone bear the financial penalty.

There are at least two insidious influences of greed upon the Christian. For one thing, it makes it easy to rationalize that we ought to have more. I remember how surprised I was when a seatmate on a plane, a fellow believer, asked me if I was into prosperity Christianity yet. I had not heard that expression before. He went on to explain that nothing is too good for a child of the King—the premise on which this concept is based.

If indeed we are sons and daughters of God—who owns the cattle on a thousand hills and to whom all the silver and gold on earth belong—then we should live like royalty, the thinking goes. For the humblest Christian, nothing is too good: the best clothes, the finest food, luxury homes—first class all the way. This philosophy is certainly inferred in the Shamanistic emphasis of Oriental Christianity and in possibility thinking of American Christianity.

This very philosophy causes some people to despair, as Patti Roberts writes in her autobiography, *Ashes to Gold*: "Seed-Faith theology bothered me a great deal because I saw that when taken to its natural extremes, it reduced God to a sugar daddy. If you wanted His blessings and His love, you paid Him off. I began to question the motivation that kind of giving implied. Were we giving to God out of love and gratitude to Him, or were we bartering with Him?"[1] There is a subtle difference between throwing ourselves before God in our need and seeking to manipulate Him through our prayers.

Some of the most enthusiastic advocates of prosperity Christianity are personal friends of mine, and I respect their right to this interpretation of Scripture. A case can be built for it in the Old Testament and in isolated passages in the New Testament. But I hold my opinion in appreciative and loving disagreement.

I know that when I seek to be like my Lord, I am following One who was a pilgrim on earth and, unlike the foxes with holes and the birds with nests, had no place to lay His head. And when He wanted to help His disciples pay their taxes, He had no money Himself but had to perform a miracle. When I read about Old Testament saints in Hebrews 11, their names stand out as if inscribed in gold. Yet, "they went about in sheepskins and goatskins, destitute, persecuted, and mistreated—the world was not worthy of them" (Heb. 11:37-38). Like them, John the Baptist, described as the greatest person born of woman (Matt. 11:11), dressed simply in camel's hair and ate only locusts and wild honey. Like them, Paul had nothing—and everything. Today, though my own personal possessions are modest, I am richer materially than all of these saints and, indeed, unworthy of them. In the light of their adversity, I have no claim to prosperity just because I am a child of the King.

A second insidious influence of greed on the Christian grows out of the feeling that we deserve everything. We become willing to compromise in order to achieve it. Integrity is often sacrificed in the pursuit of riches. While this is commonplace in the world, albeit sad, it is tragic in the church. But greed and avarice are there today also, just as in medieval times.

An outstanding operatic couple who were devoting their lives to Christian concerts had a trusted bookkeeper at home. They sent all of their receipts and billings to the office, relying on their Christian associate there. But greed entered in and embezzlement followed. Suddenly the couple on tour discovered that the records were terribly out of order, and huge sums of money were missing. It took them more than a year to straighten out their financial affairs because of the moral lapse of a fellow believer.

Or here is a large American corporation known for its strong Christian leadership. Shock waves went through the Christian community when the Canadian government accused it of falsifying custom statements and defrauding it of millions of dollars. The case was settled out of court—for $30 million!—so blame was never affixed. But the profit motive can drive us to the very edge of a moral precipice.

And, of course, some corporations have gone over the precipice. Newspaper headlines in recent years have frequently reported federal suits alleging corporate bribery to foreign nations, falsification of billings, deliberate sale of harmful products, and fraudulent inflation of charges. The bottom line is the important thing. A profit must be shown. The stock price must increase. Shareholders too are greedy and keep the pressure on. It is no doubt a good thing that directors increasingly are being held responsible for corporate decisions. Personal morality and corporate ethics cannot be kept separate. Greed invades the corporation through its people. And even Christian officers are not exempt.

Nor are Christian leaders exempt. The press made much of a television evangelist who, while he pled for contributions to his needy organization, purchased a $450,000 home and two incredibly expensive automobiles for himself. His public relations department had an explanation, but it was not easily accepted by the Christian public who felt that more was at stake than dollars.

Two of my friends have become victims of corporate bleeding. They sold their family corporations in good faith only to see them bled of all their liquid assets by the new owners and then returned through forfeiture. On the altar of money, professional relationships, personal friendships, and even family ties have been sacrificed.

The illusion of prosperity Christianity for everyone—and the temptation to achieve it by compromise—highlights a pervasive discontent among us. The Apostle John's instructions to soldiers to be satisfied with their pay could not be a norm for America (Luke 3:14). Paul's statement that he had learned to be content in all circumstances (Phil. 4:11) sounds stultifying.

While we know that "godliness with contentment is great gain" (1 Tim. 6:6), many Christians don't idealize this as a way of life. Yet in our hearts we know that merely possessing more is not enough. Mute testimony to the emptiness of material things was given by a Chicago banker. Driving to his suburban estate, he greeted his gardener and passed his cook as he went to his third-floor bedroom. There he put a revolver to his head and killed himself. All his possessions did not make life worth living.

Although we know this, many of us live in a valley of discontent and unceasingly quest for more. To the Apostle Paul, contentment meant simply being independent of circumstances. When we are in God's will, we can learn with Paul "the secret of being content in any and every situation, whether well fed or hungry, whether living in plenty or in want. I can do everything through Him who gives me strength" (Phil. 4:12-13).

Or we can learn from Christmas Evans, the eccentric Welsh evangelist who onced named his feet "Hallelujah" and "Praise the Lord." He said that wherever God led his steps, he wanted to go shouting, "Hallelujah! Praise the Lord!" For the Christian, discontentment is a sin.

Matthew 6:33 has become a life verse of mine. It was inscribed in so many gift Bibles I have received through the years that I took it as a special word from God to myself: "Seek first His kingdom and His righteousness, and all these things will be given to you as well." Out of a lifetime of experience with the Lord, I have learned to translate this text for myself, "Give the highest priority in your life to Christ Jesus and to the spiritual values of His kingdom. Then everything else will turn out all right."

When my wife, Nancy, and I were married, we chose a favorite Gospel song to be sung at our wedding. Now more than forty years later we mean it more than ever:

"All the talents I have I have laid at Thy feet, Thy approval shall be my reward; be my store great or small I have yielded it all To my wonderful, wonderful Lord."

So this is our dilemma: how are we to live out the spiritual values of first-century Christianity in the midst of twentieth-century affluence and greed?

THE RESOLUTION

It seems to me that the two kinds of people found in the Scriptures—the affluent and those with meager resources—reflect two different calls by our sovereign God. Obviously, He does not deal with us all alike.

Worldwide, most of God's children are poor and live in nations with little opportunity ever to become rich. This is not to say that it is God's will that Christians in the Western world should become poor. Nor is it His will that everyone become prosperous. Our tendency to universalize partial truth distorts the way God works uniquely with each of His children.

The Scriptures do not teach that money is a root of all kinds of evil but that the *love* of money is (1 Tim. 6:10). "The love of money" is another definition of greed. We can, in fact, be greedy when we have nothing and not be greedy when we have everything. The insatiable desire for more is a matter of heart rather than possessions, as Jesus taught in Mark 7:22.

Money itself is neutral. The love of money is not. In almost every New Testament list of personal sins, greed is mentioned: Romans 1:29; 1 Corinthians 6:10; Ephesians 5:3, 5; Colossians 3:5; 1 Timothy 3:3; 2 Timothy 3:2; 1 Peter 5:2; 2 Peter 2:14. Some persons even are described as "experts in greed."

One of Jesus' strongest warnings at this point is found in Luke 12:15: "Watch out! Be on your guard against all kinds of greed; a man's life does not consist in the abundance of his possessions."

But inspiring church history shows that Christians have been able to overcome the temptation of greed in two different ways. Some have taken voluntary vows of poverty and renounced possessions. Others have viewed all of life as a trust and dedicated their possessions for God's use. Either way offers a solution for the American dilemma.

1. *The Voluntary Abandonment of Possessions.* In 1979, when the Nobel Peace Prize Committee searched for the person who had done the most for world peace, they bypassed political figures and international statesmen to honor a 69-year-old Yugoslavian nurse in Calcutta. Since then we have become keenly aware of how a single, simple-hearted, devoted woman helped change a nation and leave a mark for good upon the entire world.

Mother Teresa received her call from God in the streets of Calcutta, where refugees were dying by the hundreds at night and their bodies being swept up like refuse in the morning. So many people. So many deaths. Who could care? One person did.

Mother Teresa began looking for dying people and for babies abandoned in garbage cans and nursed them back to health or helped them die comfortably.

"At her hands the lonely, sick, and friendless have received compassion without condescension because of her reverence for life," said the Nobel inscription.

Said Mother Teresa: "Whenever I give a piece of bread to a hungry person, I give it to Jesus."

Her beautiful prayer, with Matthew 25:35-36 in mind, about nursing the sick is in itself a declaration of love for God as the basis of Christian compassion. I used it at the inauguration of a baccalaureate nursing program at Bethel College.

> *Dearest Lord, may I see You today and every day in the person of Your sick, and whilst nursing them, minister unto You.*
>
> *Though You hide Yourself behind the unattractive disguise of the irritable, the exacting, the unreasonable, may I still recognize You and say: "Jesus, my Patient, how sweet it is to serve You."*
>
> *Lord, give me this seeing faith, then my work will never be monotonous. I will even find joy in humoring the fancies and gratifying the wishes of all poor sufferers.*
>
> *O beloved sick, how doubly dear you are to me when you personify Christ; and what a privilege is mine to be allowed to tend You.*
>
> *Sweetest Lord, make me appreciative of the dignity of my high vocation and its many responsibilities. Never permit me to disgrace it by giving way to coldness, unkindness, or impatience.*
>
> *And, O God, while You are Jesus, my Patient, deign also to be a patient Jesus, bearing with my faults, looking only to my intention, which is to love and serve You in the person of each of Your sick.*
>
> *Lord, increase my faith, bless my efforts and work now and forevermore. Amen.*[2]

No wonder Mother Teresa's statement, "Let's go and do something beautiful for God," became the inspiration for the title of her biography, *Something Beautiful for God*, by Malcolm Muggeridge. All of us have been enriched by her example.

More than 800 years ago another person lived the same kind of lifestyle of poverty and profligate self-giving as Mother Teresa. Today Francis of Assisi is also a household name. Though the son of a wealthy family, he gave up all his riches in a single act of dedication in order to rebuild Christ's church. Against the backdrop of the affluent church members and ornate churches, he led a life of poverty in itinerant preaching and compassionate ministry. Often he lived in a pigsty and always he was a beggar.

But people knew Saint Francis as a lover of God, of God's creation and God's people. He gave away his clothes to those poorer than himself. He kissed the outcast lepers whom no one loved. He spent whole nights in prayer. Within two years of his death, he was proclaimed a saint by his church, the only one honored so quickly.

Although he rarely got fifty miles outside of Assisi and died at the young age of forty-six, Saint Francis today is known by the whole world. Through Franciscans in every nation today, he is more alive than ever. Poverty did not restrict his influence for Christ.

Similarly, in Protestantism, Anglican rector David Watson established in this century a spiritual community in his home in order to advance the Lord's work through his church, Saint Michaels-le-Belfrey in York, England. Only three of the seven adults earned salaries and all lived on the earnings of those three. The others gave themselves in voluntary full-time service to Christ and to His church. They adopted personal allowances for themselves of $14 a week. To spend more than that meant that the whole community had to agree that it was God's will for a particular person to do so. I was ashamed while visiting them at the many times I had thoughtlessly spent much more than that on things of little worth. Theirs was an intense stewardship. But as a result of their dedication, and others like them in the church, a dying church was renewed in strength and became a center of nationwide spiritual renewal. Through David Watson, the whole world has been blessed and inspired.

I have been blessed by many friends who in their desire to serve Christ have chosen to possess nothing. One of them, a missionary doctor, gave up a lucrative $100,000 practice to live in a simple village on subsistence pay for himself and his family.

All of those people follow the example of C.T. Studd, who earlier in this century gave up his wealth and a promising career as a cricketer in England. Enduring long absences from his dearly loved wife, he established the Heart of Africa Holiness Mission. Today it is the Worldwide Evangelization Crusade, one of the most influential nondenominational faith missions.

In a very literal way, these people have chosen not to "store up . . . treasures on earth, where moth and rust destroy, and where thieves break in and steal . . . [but to] store up . . . treasures in heaven, where moth and rust do not destroy, and where thieves do not break in and steal" (Matt. 6:19-20). They've learned the truth of Jesus' teaching that "where your treasure is, there your heart will be also" (Matt. 6:21).

Poverty practiced by personal deep dedication for noble ends can be a world-changing force. It is not necessarily a weak base. When Kenneth Galbraith wrote *The Anatomy of Power*, he listed as the important bases of power in America: personality, wealth, and organization.[3] In the light of heroic Christians who have chosen to live with nothing, Galbraith might have added poverty as a source of power. To love Christ exclusively and not things is a source of dynamism in the world.

2. *The Investment of Possessions as a Trust.* Long before David Livingstone went to Africa as a missionary, he wrote in his diary the best definition of stewardship I've ever heard: "All that I have or possess is important to me only in its relation to Jesus Christ and His kingdom."

A new car, a suit of clothes, a new set of dishes, a hobby—all are valuable only as they somehow relate to Jesus. Stephen Neill, Anglican bishop and missionary, once described the twentieth-century Christian saint as one who has learned to bring all things into relationship to Jesus Christ.[4] Whether he has little or much, it is significant only as it points to his Saviour and Lord.

The Church of the Savior in Washington, D.C. under Donald McClanen, has developed a new mission program entitled "The Ministry of Money." Directed toward the affluent Christian, it is a call to view possessions as a trust for Christ's use in our world. My own life has been greatly enriched by many people who live by this kind of commitment.

For example, years ago while I was president of Bethel College and Seminary, I received a letter from a man who didn't even know my name. With a pencil, he had simply addressed the envelope: "Mr. President." Inside was a handwritten, four-line message and a gift of a $50,000 certificate of deposit for the school! After he got to know Bethel better, he gave additional gifts until they exceeded $1 million.

One day my wife, Nancy, and I visited him in western Minnesota. There we met a man who lived in a simpler home than our own and whose lifestyle was almost austere. Yet he had a contagious enthusiasm for life and a profound love for God.

His only regret, he told us, was that he hadn't invested his funds more wisely so that he would have had more to give to the Lord. In light of this total commitment of his means to Christ, our dedication seemed to shrink to pigmy size.

Another friend became a millionaire when the corporation he worked for went public and its stock took on significant dollar value. The shares of stock he had received from his company over many years suddenly became very valuable. He offered it all to God and spent the rest of his life finding ways to make his money contribute to Christ's work, most of the time anonymously.

Not only at Bethel but all over the world, I have seen tangible results of the dedication of his resources to the Lord's work. Whenever he made out a check to a Christian cause, he always wrote a Bible text on it: "1 Chronicles 29:14—'All things come of Thee, and of Thine own have we given Thee'" (KJV). He learned that all of God's material gifts to him were to be given back in devotion and love.

I shall never forget having breakfast one morning with another person who taught me about total dedication to Christ. At this friend's home in Sarasota, Florida, I noticed a dedication program lying on a coffee table. The program looked like many I had seen at dedications of new church sanctuaries, yet this was for a clinic.

My optometrist friend and his partners had just opened a new clinic and had invited their pastors, nurses, families, and friends to a service dedicating it to God. There they prayed that they would do a good job professionally and reflect credit upon their Lord. They prayed for opportunities to talk with patients not only about good physical sight but about spiritual vision. My friend and his colleagues own the clinic, but it belongs to God. They have given it back.

Other friends of mine have dedicated new homes, conducting house blessing services in which room by room they and the members of the family dedicated each room to God for His use. Similarly, I once sat in the front seat of a new automobile as the owner, a young engineer, thanked God for it and offered it back to Him. He prayed that the vehicle would be used for witnessing to hitchhikers, taking children to Sunday School or summer Bible camp, and running errands in Christ's service. I often thought that year when God looked down and saw all those General Motors cars moving about the city, He must have kept noticing one special car that belonged to Him.

While some saints possess nothing but have everything, others own everything yet surrender it all to God. Both groups are blessed by God and can witness with Paul, "I have learned to be content whatever the circumstances. I know what it is to be in need, and I know what it is to have plenty" (Phil. 4:11-12).

Prosperity, however, often is more damaging to the soul than adversity. Jesus warned about the paralyzing grip of wealth, insisting that it is easier for a camel to go through the eye of a needle than for a rich man to enter the kingdom of heaven. However genuine our intentions may be, it is difficult to keep investing in eternity when our funds might be used as a leverage to make more. Nor is it easy to hold everything we own lightly—like pilgrims—so we can freely expend it all in God's service. It takes a deep commitment to Christian stewardship for God to trust a saint with wealth.

At this very point, however, God's children can be the salt to preserve the twentieth-century world. British economist Barbara Ward concludes in her book *The Rich Nations and the Poor Nations* that the next great world war will not be between East and West, but between the South and North because of "the revolution of rising expectations." The have-not nations will rise against the have-nations for a more equitable distribution of the world's material goods. Already they are doing that.[5]

Stark hunger and deprivation are the basic causes of most revolutions that convulse nations today, certainly far more than Marxist ideology or political intrigue. As a result, liberation theologies have been superimposed upon the Gospel in many places. In such a world, Christians of means can demonstrate what Schaeffer termed "the compassionate use of wealth" and thus witness powerfully to needy nations. Individual philanthropy may not resolve the world's inequities. But a powerful manifestation of self-sacrificing love inspired by Christ may temper the revolt of our times.

Greed certainly will never change the world for good. But the selfless dedication of everything we have to Christ and to His people can become a revolutionary force in our time.

SIX

THE SECOND HELPING

Any serious consideration of voluntary discipline for our bodies brings us face to face with what the U.S. Public Health Service terms one of America's most serious health problems—overeating. It is not a new problem, of course. The Stone Age carving of Venus of Winlendorf depicts a noticeably plump person. The Apostle Paul wrote of Cretans whose God was their belly (Phil. 3:19). In the Medieval Ages, one of the seven deadly sins was gluttony. Today at least a third of Americans are overweight—including 50 percent of all people over age fifty-five.

A GROWING CONCERN

Scientific interest in the problems of overweight probably began in 1860 with Banting's *A Letter on Corpulence*. In the past sixty-five years, a stream of books, professional papers, and articles have been produced on the subject.

As a result, most of us know that chronic overeating can lead to serious health problems such as obesity, arteriosclerosis, diabetes, heart disease, high blood pressure, disease of the digestive system, varicose veins, breathing difficulty, and other more subtle illnesses. Certainly, Shakespeare was right when he advised in *Henry IV,* Part II, "Leave gourmandising; know the grave doth gape for thee thrice wider than for other men."

With all our knowledge, Americans still tend both to eat too much and to eat the wrong foods. Sadly, I know from personal experience. As I have aged, I have tended to become overweight. My basal metabolism has changed so that today I no longer require as much food to provide the energy I need.

Alas, I haven't learned to reduce my food intake to correspond with my energy output. Hence, at 190 pounds and 5' 9", I am among the overweight population—even after many diets and new resolves. I am learning from personal experience that professionals are right when they call for a whole new way of life to achieve proper weight control.

Being overweight is different from being obese. Overweight is anything in excess of the average on your doctor's weight charts. True, some ambiguity exists about insurance tables used to ascertain longevity. Recently, the weight levels in each age-bracket have been revised.

One flaw in the earlier weight tables was that they were based on height alone and failed to take into account the weight differences created by fatty buildup and enlarged muscular and tissue structure. Nor does the common rule of thumb calling for subtracting your waist measure from your height take this into account. According to this method, if the difference is a magic 36 or more, your weight is under control. Anything less indicates an overweight condition.

Obesity, on the other hand, consists of being more than 20 percent over the ideal body weight. Obesity is simply excessive fatness and can be defined as "a bodily state characterized by excessive collections of fatty tissues beneath the skin and within the tissue organs of the body." The fat is adipose tissue stored in the form of triglycerides.

Obesity, however, may not be the correct word to use here. It's Latin root *ob edere* literally means to "overeat." However, not all obesity is due to overeating. Obesity can also result from genetic inheritance, metabolic malfunctioning, related physical disorders and their treatments, psychological factors such as stress, and deep-seated emotional problems.

Sometimes these problems are reduced to two basic ones: metabolic obesity, a difference in the rate food is built up for storage and broken down for use; and regulatory obesity, an inability to regulate food intake. Obesity can certainly be a very complex matter.

Nevertheless, overeating is a national pastime in America because of our social lifestyle. Breakfast meetings, substantial business lunches, coffee breaks, late-evening dinners, many social occasions where additional food is served as a matter of course, and the tendency to snack while being entertained all contribute to overeating.

These social pressures, augmented by easy access to junk foods, persuasive invitations to eat by the mass media, and a general ignorance of good nutritional practices have changed the physical characteristics of Americans. During the past fifty years, children have grown 6-8 percent taller than their parents and 12-15 percent heavier. This same phenomenon is now taking place in Japan, since it has become one of the few overprivileged nations in the world.

The eating habits of Americans are on a continuum. At one extreme are those who eat too little. Among them are 1 million people afflicted with anorexia nervosa, 90 percent of them women. Many are in the unhealthy state in which their bodies are feeding cannibalistically on themselves.

At the other end of the continuum are equally ill people who splurge and purge. That is, they deliberately gorge themselves much as the Romans did before going to their vomitaria. Then, like the Romans, these modern counterparts empty their stomachs by means of vomiting, enemas, or suppositories. Those who just splurge simply continue to add weight, and a few people in America have exceeded a thousand pounds; though not necessarily wholly as a result of intemperance.

Perhaps Epstein's 1882 characterization of obesity's three stages may still be true: enviable, comical, pitiable.

Most overweight Americans are somewhere between the two extremes. Their primary problems cluster around too much food, too little exercise, and excessive stress. A wealth of educational information is available about all three topics. Information alone, however, is not sufficient to trigger rigorous self-discipline. A special kind of commitment is needed.

PLUMP CHRISTIANS AND THE BIBLE

Concern for proper weight characterizes not only Americans generally but Christians specifically. I have often noted the trimness of chief executive officers at management seminars. I contrasted that with the not-so-trim figures of many Christian organizational leaders, including myself.

I concluded that the Christian leader's sense of personal discipline about eating doesn't match that of the secular leader. Today, however, "Christians are into the lean look," as Ron Enroth wrote in a review of diet programs led by Christians for Christians.[1] While rapid weight-loss schemes are no permanent cure for most people, the quickened interest in good physical tonus gives hope for a new generation of firm leaders in the future.

The Bible contains a high view of the Christian's body. Through the resurrection, God gave an eternal dimension to the human body: "The Lord Jesus . . . will transform our lowly bodies so that they will be like His glorious body" (Phil. 3:20-21). Greek dualism is not found in the Scriptures—the body deprecated as evil and the spirit respected because it alone is pure. We are a fusion of body and soul meant to exist inseparably forever. The body, in fact, is the individuating principle of the soul. Hence, many Scripture passages encourage us to pay heed to our bodies in this life: "Offer your bodies as living sacrifices" (Rom. 12:1). "Your body is a temple of the Holy Spirit" (1 Cor. 6:19). "I beat my body and make it my slave" (1 Cor. 9:27). "Each of you should learn to control his own body" (1 Thes. 4:4). "Physical training is of some value" (1 Tim. 4:8). " 'Food for the stomach and the stomach for food'—but God will destroy them both. The body is . . . for the Lord, and the Lord for the body" (1 Cor. 6:13).

Perhaps the highest ideal for a Christian view of eating is found in 1 Corinthians 10:31: "So whether you eat or drink or whatever you do, do it all for the glory of God." The way we eat and what we eat is meant to contribute ultimately to God's glory!

THE "WELLNESS" EMPHASIS

Proper care of the body is but one facet of a broader holistic concept known as "wellness." The philosophy undergirding this approach is attributed to botanist Jan Smuts, who taught that the determining factors in nature are wholes, such as organisms, and not their constituent parts.

Wellness centers have sprung up all over the nation to encourage a preventative maintenance approach to health. To prevent problems from developing, people visit the centers regularly.

Physical well-being is only part of the wellness approach. Summarized by Donald B. Ardell in his book *High Level Wellness,* holistic medicine is defined as "viewing a person and his/her wellness from every possible perspective, taking into account every available concept and skill for the person's growth toward harmony and balance. It means treating the person and not the disease. And it promotes the interrelationship of body, mind, and spirit." He lists five foundational dimensions for wellness:

1. Self-responsibility
2. Nutritional awareness
3. Stress management
4. Physical fitness
5. Environmental sensitivity[2]

In *Body Mind,* Don Ethan Miller describes total fitness as "the ability to function at an optimum level in all daily living. This encompasses the whole philosophy of the science of health—intellectual, emotional, and social—as well as physical conditioning. A totally fit individual has the strength, speed, agility, endurance and social and emotional adjustment appropriate to his age."[3] Dr. Miller concludes that the vast majority of people today are living at only a fraction of their potential.

The wellness concept has many implications for Christian living, including the interrelationship of body and soul, development of purpose for life, acceptance of responsibility for personal initiative, sharpening of religious values to motivate behavior modification, and the quest for optimum fitness in each phase of life.'

John J. Pilch, in his book *Wellness: An Introduction to a Full Life,* sees a direct tie between wellness and spirituality. To him spirituality "is that aspect of a person's relationship with spiritual reality which seeks to develop and perfect the human spirit with, and never in neglect of, the body and its senses."

The task of any authentic spirituality, in his judgment, "is to increasingly integrate the sensuous into the whole person so that it is directed by good decisions and ordered to God. A spirituality that is not sensuous is not authentic."[4]

Wellness centers usually are not medical clinics. People are referred to others when medicine or surgery is indicated as necessary. Neither are they "fat" clinics for overcoming weight problems.

DISCIPLINE A KEY

Despite all these helps, it must be remembered that the only effective approach to weight loss is a lifelong, systematic, permanent change in eating habits. Disciplined eating habits are not easy to maintain.

"Of all human frailties," wrote Judith Rudin, "obesity is perhaps the most perverse. Its penalities are so severe, the gratifications so limited, and the remedy so simple that obesity should be the most trivial of aberrations to correct, yet it is the most recalcitrant. Almost any person can lose weight. Few can keep it off."[5]

Dr. Albert Stunkard made the same observation in 1971 when he concluded that "most obese persons will not remain in treatment. Of those who do remain in treatment, most will not lose much weight, and of those who do lose weight, most will regain it."[6]

In some research, only about 10 percent of patients in supervised weight reduction programs maintained their original losses for as long as one year. After two years, the total dropped to 6 percent, then even lower. Another report revealed that reducing diets have a five-year failure rate of 98 to 99 percent. No wonder the National Association to Aid Fat Americans (NAAFA) was incorporated in 1969. Its purpose is to give reinforcement to people who feel they function better somewhat heavy and to fight discriminatory practices against obese people.

Out of America's growing consciousness of its need for physical fitness, many programs have emerged directed by Christian enthusiasts which offer nutritional guidance and/or regular exercise. Some are even set to music! These include such intriguingly named enterprises as Diet, Discipline, Discipleship—a program related to the Community of Jesus on Cape Cod that has been tried by 100,000 people in 5,000 churches; the Blessercise program of Marie Chapain; Praise-R-Cise of Joey and Bernadette Di Francisca;

Shape Up of Nancy Larson; Shape Up America Seminars of Bob and Yvonne Turnbull; Believercise of Cathi Stout; Devotion in Motion of Joan Hake Robie; and the Aerobics Program for Total Well Being of Kenneth Cooper. None of these people advocate fad diets.

Beyond the foundational approaches to weight control—diet, exercise, and stress reduction—more serious treatments are available for obesity: psychoanalysis, interactional psychotherapy, behavior approaches, multimodal behavior treatment, group therapy, hypnotherapy and drugs. Ultimately, however, a permanent change in weight will be the result of a permanent change in attitude toward eating which leads to a permanent change in lifestyle.

This changed attitude will include appreciation of nutritional values, readiness to monitor and correct eating practices, willingness to live on the edge of hunger, commitment to living by principle rather than by impulse or pressure, and a deep-seated desire to glorify God through one's body. Weight control is hard work. That's why so many give up.

None of the following easy slogans makes a difference: "Be thin to be in" / "He who indulges, bulges" / "You can lead a person to cottage cheese but you can't make him shrink" / "I want to see less of you" / "The vanishing Americans."

Charlie Shedd, in his book *The Fat Is in Your Head*, does suggest a slogan that applies very well: "I want to live with You today, Lord." God's response is, "It's a date! Meet Me on the hill!"[7] At the place of self-crucifixion, we win our victories.

There are times when the Christian may choose to turn down not only the second helping but the first helping also. There may be good reasons for doing this, but one that is receiving more attention by believers today is the fast for religious reasons. The Bible does not speak of dieting as such, but it makes much mention of fasting—a spiritual exercise with healthful side effects. The New Testament word for fasting simply means "not to eat." The Old Testament word means "affliction of the soul" as a result of voluntarily not eating.

Christians fasting thus may be defined as abstaining from eating for a time because of a religious motive. Although fasting for spiritual purposes has fallen out of much evangelical church practice, it has not fallen out of the Scriptures.

CONSIDER FASTING

Perhaps at a time when Christians are looking at the care of their physical bodies as a spiritual trust from God, we ought to revive the ancient custom of fasting. If others today make use of it for nonphysical reasons—students on college campuses to identify with world hunger, prisoners in Ireland to protest their nation's division, idealistic young people to lash out at the war machinery, Gandhi to bring the British Empire to its knees—why should not Christians employ fasting for its spiritual values?

The values of fasting were well summed up by the sixteenth-century Christian mystic Francis de Sales when he counseled: "If you are able to fast, you will do well . . . for in addition to the ordinary benefits of fasting, namely elevation of the spirit, subduing the flesh, strengthening virtue . . . it is a great matter to command our tastes and inclinations, and to keep the body and appetites subject to the law of the spirit."[8]

Specifically, fasting can be soul-strengthening in the following ways:

1. *Fasting dramatizes our confession of sin.* The Old Testament is replete with persons who accompanied their confessions of sin by fasting. The Apostle John's trilogy of entering points for temptation—the lust of the flesh, the lust of the eyes, and the pride of life, (1 John 2:16, KJV)—includes the body. Fasting serves as a physical remonstrance for the body, whose instinctive behaviors often lead to sin. Fasting is appropriate to accompany heartfelt confession of failure to God.

2. *Fasting evidences mastery over the body.* Because the hunger instinct is so powerful, when we refuse to satisfy it, we show that life's ultimate control center is the spirit, not the flesh. Delayed satisfaction is needed to counteract the hedonism of our times. Fasting, then, is intensified self-discipline.

3. *Fasting intensifies awareness of God's presence.* Fasting quickens our faith—our sixth intuitive sense—and makes the unseen spiritual world real to us, just as our five physical senses make us conscious of the material world.

Anglican bishop Stephen Neill once said that one mark of a twentieth-century saint is his or her ability to live at home in a world that cannot be seen.[9] Fasting enriches prayer—conversation with God—and in the Scriptures often accompanies prayer.

4. *Fasting focuses life upon ultimate issues.* Radical change in a normal way of life opens the door to reflection upon life's meaning. In such crises as an auto accident, the death of a loved one, or the loss of a job, we experience this clarity. It can happen also in the noncrisis experience of fasting. Time out from the ordinary promotes thought about the extraordinary. Most of us are so busy in our activist Western world that we need to stop occasionally to think about why we engage in so much activity and for what purpose.

5. *Fasting empowers the soul for special tasks.* Fasting is a form of spiritual adrenalin. Bringing into focus God's call to special service and the omnipotent power available to us through His Spirit, fasting is strategic preparation to carry out new responsibilities for Christ. As Christ fasted in the wilderness prior to selecting the twelve disciples, and as they fasted before beginning their missionary journeys, so Christians today can employ fasting to prepare their hearts for new endeavors of faith. We then learn in a profound way Jesus' teaching that man does not live by bread alone.

All of these values of fasting are for our own soul improvement. Nowhere in the Scriptures are we encouraged to fast to manipulate God or to seek to employ Him for our ends. Fasting grows out of an inner response to God's initiative. In the process, we become better people and more usable for His purposes. Happily, if the physical purging effect of a fast improves our bodies also, that's simply a plus which makes them keener instruments in God's hands.

In the Bible, the length of fasts vary greatly. The longest were forty days—Jesus in the wilderness (Matt. 4:1) and Moses receiving the Law (Deut. 9:9). Daniel fasted for three weeks in Persia when he lamented the revelation God had given him (Dan. 10:2).

Three-day fasts were observed by Paul after his conversion (Acts 9:9) and by Queen Esther before she brought her petition for the Jews to the king (Es. 4:16). Other fasts lasted only one day—David mourning the death of Saul and Jonathan (2 Sam. 1:12) and Israel preparing for battle with Benjamin (Jud. 20:26). Some fasts were only for one meal, such as that observed by the church before commissioning its new missionaries (Acts 13:3).

While the New Testament has no commandment about Christians needing to fast as a religious exercise, it seems to be assumed that they will do so. The Old Testament shows that Israel developed a significant distinction between religious feasting and religious fasting.

Jesus Himself implied the value of fasting when He talked about its appropriateness for Christians when their Bridegroom is physically absent from them (Matt. 9:15). In the Sermon on the Mount, Christ linked fasting with almsgiving and prayer and stressed in their practice to please God and not people (Matt. 6:16-18).

Individual fasting, in fact, is to be concealed from friends and observed only before the Lord. So also is individual prayer and deeds of love. Thus, the spiritual value of these religious exercises is preserved. A voluntary observance will be much more meaningful than a legalistic approach ever could be.

Voluntary fasting ceased in the sixteenth century through a proscription at the Council of Orleans. It then became obligatory. In later centuries, however, fasting was subject to such ascetic extremism and empty ritualism that many Christians turned from it altogether. In this new age of the Spirit, a return to voluntary fasting as an aid to devotion to God is once again in order.

Many Christians are leading the way. In South Korea, where many prayer mountains exist, the Central Full Gospel Church of Seoul maintains a prayer-fasting mountain twenty-five miles outside the city. There, thousands of believers may be found fasting on any day, some spending three days to three weeks in fasting and praying. This is duplicated in many other Korean churches. Many church leaders believe this phenomenon is the secret of the spiritual vitality of the Korean church, as well as its amazing numerical growth and its recent emergence as a missionary training and sending nation. Certainly, corporate fasting forges a deep bond of spiritual unity and concern.

In our own country, the charismatic movement has been accompanied by religious fasts which have had a strong spiritual impact upon its adherents and the rest of the Christian church. Many retreat centers of the nation make fasting a regular part of their spiritual renewal programs.

Contemporary advocates of fasting as a spiritual exercise find helpful support in John Wesley, the founder of Methodism. Not only did he fast personally twice a week, but he encouraged his followers to make it a regular practice. His primary concern was not for the mortification of the flesh—he deplored that—but for the concentration of more time in personal communion with God. While he acknowledged many spiritual benefits from fasting, its overall purpose was "that it be done unto the Lord, with our eye singly fixed on Him. Let our intention herein be this, and this alone, to glorify our Father which is in heaven."[10]

New voices, like Richard Foster, are being heard in our time, sounding a compelling call to return to biblically centered fasting as an appropriate spiritual exercise for twentieth-century believers. Foster also insists that such fasting must center on God and be God-initiated and God-ordained. He recognizes other benefits— physical well-being, success in prayer, endowment with power, spiritual insights—but "these must never replace God as the center of our fasting."[11]

For those who become interested in the practical matters related to fasting—how to begin, how to continue, and how to conclude— there are many specific helpful suggestions in Arthur Wallis' book *God's Chosen Fast*[12] reprinted many times since it was first issued in 1968. Foster deals with some of these matters also.

SETTING AN EXAMPLE

All of this may well lead us to exemplify a larger ideal expressed by John Calvin, the cerebral leader of the Reformation who said: "The life of the faithful, indeed, ought to be so regulated by frugality and sobriety as to exhibit as far as possible the appearance of a perpetual fast."[13]

Saying no to the second helping may be one of our most effective responses to Mooneyham's question: "What can we say to a hungry world?"[14] When more than half the world goes to bed hungry at night, overeating in the few overprivileged nations is not just a physical problem. It may well be a moral problem also.

To be sure, our individual restraint will not solve the nutritional needs of the hungry world. But it will set an example. In chapter 5 I referred to British economist Barbara Ward, who insists that the next world conflict will result from poverty and hunger. A heroic example by Christians of the North may possess enough dynamic power to temper that.

Just as Abraham Lincoln insisted in the nineteenth century that our nation could no longer exist half slave and half free, so our twentieth-century world can no longer exist half hungry and half well-fed. Poverty and hunger, more than Marxism, is the cause of today's revolutions among nations.

Of course, we also must do more to make our economic and political systems reflect Judaeo-Christian compassion for hungry people everywhere. We can make a point to set personal examples of self-discipline that may release a new moral dynamism as a counterforce to injustice in the world.

SEVEN

ALTERNATIVE SEXUAL PRACTICES

Recently my assistant brought to my office *Equal Time News,* a widely circulated newspaper for the gay community which she had picked up in the St. Paul skyway system. As I took a moment to peruse it, I noticed that the lead article spoke of a year of firsts for the Minneapolis City Council. For the first time women occupy a majority of council seats, and the term *councilmen* has been changed to council members. Also for the first time, an admitted homosexual fills a council seat.

The letters to the editor caught my attention. One person commented: "I have often wondered why whenever there was some presentation of a gay issue in the media, some sober-faced guardian of morality would be presented afterward to offer an archaic *scriptural* condemnation of whatever gay issue was presented. Now I know why. The public is really interested in what the churches have to say. The church stands opposed, always, heroically, on the side of the status quo."[1]

THE BIBLICAL VIEW

On the subject of alternative sexual practices, perhaps it's helpful to look at what the letter writer would call an "archaic" scriptural passage, 1 Corinthians 6:9-11, in which Paul speaks straightforwardly—"Do you not know that the wicked will not inherit the kingdom of God? Do not be deceived: Neither the sexually immoral nor idolators nor adulterers nor male prostitutes nor homosexual offenders nor thieves nor the greedy nor drunkards nor slanderers will inherit the kingdom of God. And this is what some of you were."

If you refer to 1 Corinthians 1:2 (kjv), you'll see that there is hope for these people In spite of their immoral background, they are addressed as saints. And this is our hope also. Our sins may be different from theirs, but the promise is for us all: "You were washed, you were sanctified, you were justified in the name of the Lord Jesus Christ by the Spirit of our God" (1 Cor. 6:11).

Hence, any forthright confrontation with immorality must be carried out against the background of God's unconditional love for all people, His readiness to forgive any sin, and His desire to impart strength for a new life. We must be incarnations of His understanding and acceptance even as we seek to uphold His standards. Only then will we be like our Saviour when He responded to the adulterous women, "Neither do I condemn you. . . . Go now and leave your life of sin!" (John 8:11) To call sin a sin in a nonjudgmental spirit is one of the challenges of our day. In part, such an approach grows out of an appreciation for the complexities of people's problems, the pressures of urban life, and the moral drift of society as a whole. As we recognize the bias toward evil in all of us, we will be most helpful by acknowledging at least inwardly, "There but for the grace of God go I."

Because Rome and Corinth in Paul's time were not unlike Chicago or New York City in ours, Paul's directness with the Romans can be instructive for us. Paul's letter to the Romans was written from Corinth, where he spent a year and a half. He had ample opportunity to observe the people's conduct in that wicked city. He laments in Romans 1:24-27: "Therefore God gave them over in the sinful desires of their hearts to sexual impurity for the degrading of their bodies with one another. They exchanged the truth of God for a lie, and worshiped and served created things rather than the Creator—who is forever praised. Amen.

"Because of this, God gave them over to shameful lusts. Even their women exchanged natural relationships for unnatural ones. In the same way the men also abandoned natural relations with

women and were inflamed with lust for one another. Men committed indecent acts with other men, and received in themselves the
due penalty for their perversion."

Corinth was probably the most immoral city in Greece. An urban
center varying from 100,000 to 500,000 people, and the capital of
Achaia, it was a transit city of sailors, businessmen, and traveling
governmental officials.

The worship of Venus, the love goddess, was common. On the
Acropolis was the Temple of Aphrodite. Here a thousand religious
prostitutes were on duty, at night plying their trade on the streets
among sailors and businessmen. New prostitutes were added by
businessmen who sought success by offering as temple gifts wom-
en they had brought from other parts of the world.

Homosexuality also was very common in Corinth. Of the first
fifteen Roman emperors, fourteen were homosexual. Author William Barclay, renowned New Testament scholar, reports that Em-
peror Nero castrated one young man, married him in a full ceremo-
ny, and lived with him as his wife. At the same time Nero also
married a man he called his husband.

These degraded forms of life were surrounded by all kinds of
beauty and culture. Some of the world's loveliest architecture
came from the Greeks. We still replicate the Corinthian columns
on our national buildings whenever we can afford to do so. Corinth
was a city of pottery, art, and ceramics. An often-filled odeum
seated 3,000 people for plays, musical performances, and other
cultural presentations. An amphitheater accommodated 20,000
people. Great culture coexisted with great degradation in the city.

Shortly after World War II, an abandoned mansion was discovered in the mountains of Germany. Hanging in its rooms were
some of the great original works of art. Clearly, someone had
enjoyed fine things. The mansion had been the home of Heinrich
Himmler, chiefly responsible for murdering 6 million Jews. As in
Corinth, here in the mansion, the enjoyment of culture coexisted
with the planning of evil deeds.

Culture doesn't make us good people. Education doesn't make us
good people. Civilization doesn't make us good people. Corinth
was a mute witness to the truth that loveliness can surround us
even while we are degraded in our souls.

William Baird has written a helpful book *The Corinthian Church,
a Biblical Approach to Urban Culture*. He speaks of five fundamental Corinthian problems which still are major concerns in any
urban culture: divisions, morality, secularism, worship, and death.[2]

Certainly, morality is as fundamental a problem in our large
metropolitan centers today as it was in first-century Rome and
Corinth. Paul suggests two appropriate Christian responses to the
immoral use of human bodies: "'Everything is permissible for
me'—but not everything is beneficial. 'Everything is permissible for
me'—but I will not be mastered by anything. 'Food for the stomach
and the stomach for food'—but God will destroy them both. The
body is not meant for sexual immorality, but for the Lord, and the
Lord for the *body*" (1 Cor. 6:12-13, emphasis added).

I understand Paul to say here that just because it is perfectly
legal before the Law to satisfy hunger for food by eating any time
you desire, it does not follow that it is perfectly legal before God to
satisfy the instincts of sex any time and in any way. As Paul writes:
"By His power, God raised the Lord from the dead, and He will
raise us also. Do you not know that your *bodies* are members of
Christ Himself? Shall I then take the members of Christ and unite
them with a prostitute? Never! Do you not know that he who
unites himself with a prostitute is one with her in *body?* For it is
said, 'The two will become one flesh.' But he who unites himself
with the Lord is one with Him in Spirit.

"Flee from sexual immorality. All other sins a man commits are
outside his *body,* but he who sins sexually sins against his own
body. Do you not know that your *body* is a temple of the Holy
Spirit, who is in you, whom you have received from God? You are
not your own; you are bought at a price. Therefore honor God with
your *body*" (1 Cor. 6:14-20, emphasis added).

Here Paul teaches two Christian responses to the prevailing
immoral use of the body. Flee sexual immorality. Honor God with
your body.

FLEE SEXUAL IMMORALITY
The Greek word for sexual immorality is
porneo, from which we get our word pornography. Minnesota
philosopher Dr. Willard Herberg observes, "The moral crises of our

time consist primarily not in widespread violation of accepted moral standards—when has any age been free of that?—but in the repudiation of these very moral standards themselves. The very notion of morality or a moral code seems to be losing its meaning for increasing numbers of men and women in our society."[3]

Our big problem in America just now is exactly this—our moral code is losing its meaning. A Christian America never existed, but there was a time when non-Christians respected the biblical moral code as an ideal, whether or not they subscribed to it. In our pluralistic society, the moral consensus is gone.

Today we live as they did in the days of Judges, when everyone did what seemed right in his own eyes. We have no common moral code. God has established His standards, but we do not own them. Nevertheless, the seventh commandment, "Thou shalt not commit adultery," is what Edith Schaeffer describes as still one of our crucial *Lifelines*.[4]

Jesus takes the seventh commandment of Deuteronomy 5 and interprets it more strictly, saying: "You have heard that it was said, 'Do not commit adultery.' But I tell you that anyone who looks at a woman lustfully has already committed adultery with her in his heart. If your right eye causes you to sin, gouge it out and throw it away" (Matt. 5:27-29).

Of course this is a hyperbole, but it also is a powerful expression of speech describing the need to flee sexual immorality. "And if your right hand causes you to sin, cut it off and throw it away. It is better for you to lose one part of your body than for your whole body to go into hell" (Matt. 5:30).

Paul adds: "But among you there must not be even a hint of sexual immorality, or of any kind of impurity, or of greed, because these are improper for God's holy people. Nor should there be obscenity, foolish talk, or coarse joking, which are out of place, but rather thanksgiving. For of this you can be sure: No immoral, impure, or greedy person—such a man is an idolater—has any inheritance in the kingdom of Christ and of God. Let no one deceive you with empty words" (Eph. 5:3-6).

So the seventh commandment in Deuteronomy 5, Jesus' interpretation in Matthew 5, and Paul's application in Ephesians 5 all reveal a moral standard for the world. But in place of that standard today, we have such guidelines as *Playboy* magazine, Hugh Hefner's contribution to what twenty years ago was called the new morality.

Hefner taught that pleasure is a basic principle, living in sin is not sin, and more or less anything goes between consenting adults. Summarizing in the *Chicago Sun-Times* last year, columnist Justin Smith said that the *Playboy* philosophy consists of two basic outlooks: (1) sex outside of marriage isn't just all right; it is desirable because sex without marriage is a lot of fun; (2) the individual and his self-gratification is just about the most important thing in the world.[5]

In one form or another, in America these outlooks have taken precedence over Deuteronomy 5, Matthew 5, and Ephesians 5. In fact, it is reported that Hefner once boasted: "If Christ were here today and had to choose between being on the staff of *Playboy* magazine or being on the staff of one of the joy-killing, pleasure-denying churches, He would, of course, immediately join *Playboy*."[6]

In modern America, at least eight prevailing forms of sexual immorality can be identified from which we need to flee:

1. *Casual sex.* Sometimes this is called recreational sex. The Allen Healthmocker Institute estimates that 80 percent of all male teenagers and 66 percent of all female teenagers are sexually active. This means four of every five teenage fellows and two of every three teenage girls.

Some researchers say that only one person in ten enters marriage today as a virgin. One of ten adolescent girls becomes pregnant each year. Four of every ten get pregnant in their teens and half will get abortions, according to U.S. Senator Jeremiah Denton of Alabama.

The director of the Center for Disease Control in Atlanta concludes that no one has ever lived in an era more conducive to sexually transmitted disease. Twenty different venereal diseases now exist in addition to gonorrhea and syphilis. Five million people have herpes right now—200,000 new cases a year—and no cure exists, as far as we know. Predictably, a tenth of all women will become sterile by 1990 as a result of these diseases.

2. *Cohabitation.* The 1982 census reveals that the number of

unmarried people living together is still climbing. A total of 1.9 million unmarried couples cohabit in America. It is now an acceptable alternative lifestyle. Many cities have passed human rights legislation making it impossible for a landlord to deny an apartment to two unmarried people who choose to live together.

One of the many predicaments that can result from cohabitation was evident in a letter to *Dear Abby*:

"My boyfriend and I live together and because of a previous bad marriage (mine) we have decided not to include marriage in our future. However, we would like to have children. I'm afraid that my company would frown upon motherhood without marriage, but I feel that I am within my rights to have a child if it will be brought up in a stable, loving home. We've considered saying we are married to ensure company approval, but we prefer to be honest. If we choose to have a family, can I be legally terminated for this reason? I can't afford to jeopardize my career."

Abby replied quite directly: "If you can't afford to jeopardize your career, I advise you to live according to society's prevailing rules and get married before having a family."

To flee sexual immorality includes fleeing cohabitation.

3. *Sequential polygamy*. This refers to frequent divorces—not the occasional divorce for which many churches carry out redemptive ministries but multiple divorces.

An actress in the television show "Gunsmoke" married for the *fifth* time. Fifty-two years old, she'd been married so many times that she didn't want another ring. So her groom, a man from Texas, gave her a horse instead!

A Guiness record was broken in 1984 when a seventy-seven-year-old man married his twenty-seventh wife! In the days of the Roman Empire, one citizen commented about a Roman woman who was marrying her tenth husband: "I am offended less by a prostitute who is straightforward than by a person marrying her tenth husband."

To flee sexual immorality is to flee sequential polygamy.

4. *Adultery*. Four sex researchers—Kinsey, Hite, and Masters and Johnson—report similarly about adultery. They conclude that a third to half of the American husbands and a fourth to a third of wives engage in extramarital affairs. As I mentioned earlier, a new

area for adultery is the executive suite, where women have won the battle for equal rights in their climb up the corporate ladder.

More and more top-level executives are having extramarital love affairs with each other. One woman consultant advised in a recent national magazine that when two corporate officers engage in an affair, they should not continue together in the organization. For the morale of the organization, one must go and, she concludes it should be the woman.

"We're seeing more extramarital activity and therapists are helping people to accommodate this sexual behavior without destroying the marriage and family," reported Donald Granville, a social work professor at the University of Texas after a survey of 262 therapists. Not only did he find adulterous relationships among the clients, he reported, but of the therapists surveyed, 40 percent confessed that they had at least one extramarital experience themselves![7]

To flee sexual immorality includes fleeing adultery.

5. *Prostitution*. Dr. William S. Banowski, professor of philosophy at Pepperdine College, declares: "Prostitution is evil because it degrades the prostitute and reduces her to an object to be used, not a person to be respected in her own right."[8] Not all prostitution is sleazy. That was evidenced by the cultured college graduate who directed her own call-girl program in New York City. It was all tastefully done in high fashion and the stakes were high—sometimes $2,500 for one alliance. In the end, however, the life deteriorates. As the prostitute grows older and loses some of her youthful beauty, she begins to work later and more dangerous hours for less pay. One social worker commented, "I've been amazed at the number of bag ladies I work with who are former prostitutes. Now they have nothing to sell and no future."[9]

I am glad for the inspiring example of Temple Baptist Church, Portland, Oregon, a downtown church which is reaching out to help prostitutes in the inner city. In a nonjudgmental way, church members have opened their hearts and homes to help young women escape the degradation they've been trapped in. In a very literal sense, the church is helping them flee sexual immorality.

But Temple Baptist is only one church. Probably as many as 120,000 teenagers are selling sex in New York City alone. The

National Task Force on Prostitution estimates that there are more than a million adult prostitutes in the United States today. In addition, every major city has a supply of business-related call girls. Of the men who patronize them, 95 percent have wives, but their marriages are in trouble.[10]

6. *Mental masturbation.* This is a more graphic term for the effects of pornography. The Supreme Court definition of pornography has always been ambiguous and difficult to apply: "That which offends contemporary standards of taste, is without scientific, cultural, political, or literary value, is without redeeming social significance and which appeals to the prurient interests."

Citizens of Minneapolis were disturbed when their mayor vetoed a pornography ordinance passed by the city council. The ordinance ruled that pornography is a violation of human rights for women and the First Amendment of the United States Constitution. If passed, the bill would have closed many places of pornography in the city.

Esther Waltenberg, professor in the University of Minnesota School of Social Work, defended the ordinance, saying, "Pornography is not an expression of freedom of speech but a violation of the civil rights of women. Pornography is not a celebration of sexual freedom nor the innocent arena of bawdy fun. It is the cynical exploitation of obscene smut with women and increasingly children as the victims."[11]

What is pornography? Currently, it is defined in four different gradations: (1) general sexual materials in which no explicit sex organs are pictured; (2) marginal erotica in which sex organs are exposed in pictures; (3) erotica, the depiction in pictures of sexual acts, and (4) hard-core erotica with live or filmed performances of sexual acts.

Pornography in these forms appears in magazines, books, films, video cassettes, and slides. Increasingly, it is being run on television. Dial-a-porn advertised phone numbers also give recorded obscene messages. Live sex shows are big business. It is estimated that pornography was a $7 billion business in 1984 in the U.S. That is equal to the combined volume done by the "conventional" movie and record business.[12] Organized crime has moved deeply into marketing it. Wherever there are easy dollars, crime follows.

The ten leading sex magazines in the country together take in $475 million a year. *Playboy* reaches an estimated 12 million homes. In addition, 800 "adult" theaters report through their trade association that they have 3 million admissions a week and gross half a billion dollars annually.[13] There are three times as many adult book stores as McDonald's Golden Arches—15,000 in all, or about twenty in every major city and one in almost every minor city.

St. Paul, Minnesota took a significant step recently when after years of failing to control downtown pornographic displays and adult peep shows, the city council simply bought out the owner. He was paid $1.5 million for his downtown buildings and asked to sign an agreement not to set up business again in St. Paul.

How harmful is pornography? A study reported by the *Arizona Republic* newspaper revealed a close correlation between rapes and sales of sex magazines per capita. Alaska is number one in rapes—72 for every 100,000 people—and number one in per capita sales of sex magazines, the "gentlemen's sophisticates" as they're called.

Nevada is number two both in rapes and in sales of pornographic magazines. California, Arizona, and Colorado all are in the top ten in rape and sex magazine sales. An editorial in the *Arizona Republic* insisted that the correlation is more than chance.[14] Similarly, researchers at the University of Wisconsin and UCLA have found that exposure to pornography, particularly sex linked with violence, motivates some 35 percent of male viewers to violent acts against women.[15]

Of increasing concern is child pornography. Scores of pornographic magazines exploit children, having such titles as *Tiny Nudes, Call Boys, Little Beavers,* and *Lollitots.* In America, 1.2 million children ages eight to fifteen are involved in sex for sale. Every year a million from ages one to sixteen are molested and filmed.[16] In 1984 a large private school in California to which unsuspecting parents took their children was discovered to be a center of vicious child pornography.

To flee sexual immorality means we must flee from mental masturbation—pornography.

7. *Homosexuality.* Joan Scherer Brewer of the Kinsey Institute estimates that 10 percent of the male population in the United

States has had extensive homosexual experience. The institute counts anyone a homosexual who has had six experiences with another person of the same sex.[17] Recently, the National Council of Churches debated the question of homosexuality in Vancouver in connection with a motion to admit into membership a gay church. The recommendation was narrowly defeated.

Two popular evangelical writers currently advocate that evangelicals support the gay Christian movement to let homosexuals know they can accept Christ and still be homosexuals. They insist we not only are to love homosexuals but should accept them.

In this matter, I have been guided largely by Louis Smedes' book *Sex for Christians*. He relates three basic principles to 1 Corinthians 7: (1) Sexuality is meant to be woven into the whole character and integrated into our quest for human values. (2) Sexuality is meant to be an urge toward a deep relationship with another person. (3) Sexuality is meant to move toward a heterosexual relationship of love—not a homosexual one.[18]

Dr. Irving Bieber, associate clinical professor at New York Medical College, also has contributed to my thinking. In an older, controversial study, he and his colleagues concluded that homosexuality is not a normal variant of sexuality. He writes: "In our judgment, a heterosexual shift is a possibility for all homosexuals who are strongly motivated to change. We assume that heterosexuality is the biological norm and that, unless interfered with, all individuals are heterosexual. Homosexuals do not bypass heterosexual development phases and all remain potentially heterosexual."[19]

Friends of mine close to this field of study disagree with this conclusion. A great deal of controversy exists over whether it is nature (genes and chromosomes) or nurture (environment) that leads people into homosexuality.

Sex researchers Masters and Johnson believe that homosexuality is entirely a learned phenomenon without any physiological base. They assert that children are born sexually neutral and get channeled one way or another by various learning experiences.[20] Kinsey reported a 65 percent success ratio with 67 homosexuals he sought to return to heterosexuality, indicating that a shift is possible.

Whether homosexuality is an ingrained physiological variant or a learned pattern of behavior that can be changed, the grace of God is able to do two things for a homosexual: (1) help the person shift to heterosexuality, or (2) keep the individual chaste in spite of homosexual tendencies.

We need to respond to the gay movement much as Lot responded to homosexuality in his day. His deep feelings are recorded in 2 Peter 2:7: And God "rescued Lot, a righteous man, who was distressed by the filthy lives of lawless men (for that righteous man, living among them day after day, was tormented in his righteous soul by the lawless deeds he saw and heard)."

Other translations say Lot was "horrified" or "sickened" in his soul. In our time we have gotten so used to homosexuality that I'm afraid we no longer are repulsed by what is happening in America.

To flee sexual immorality is to flee homosexuality.

8. *Incest.* We've learned much more about incest in the past eight years because, as with the gay movement, it has come out of the closet. Only recently have we discovered incest to be a serious national problem.

What is incest? It is sexual intercourse, or devious sexual relationships between individuals closely related by blood. When parents are involved sexually with their children, it is considered aggravated incest. Much incest does not reach the point of actual intercourse, but involves almost everything else.

How common is it? Based on interviews with 795 coeds in New England, 19 percent of all women now in college and 9 percent of all men have been victims of childhood incest.[21] One child in every ten families is a likely candidate for incest.[22] Linda Kohl, a staff writer for the St. Paul *Dispatch*, estimates on the basis of her research that 15-20 percent of women in the U.S. have been incest victims.[23]

The average age of the victim is between five and ten years. When asked about the experience, children tend to say they were ignorant or that their partner told them it was the way everybody expressed love. Consequently, they entered the act innocently.

A *Cosmopolitan* magazine survey of 100,000 women disclosed that 11 percent had experienced incest as a child. In San Jose, California 5 percent of the city's grade-school girls are in court-ordered therapy because of sexual exploitation, mostly incest.

Dr. David Finkelhor, director of the University of New Hampshire Family Violence Project, writes strongly: "I think 99 percent of the men who commit incest know that it is wrong, and they are no more deserving of empathy than bank robbers."

One major problem is that incest leaves a psychological time bomb. The confusion and guilt that develops in a child grows as the child matures and often explodes later into promiscuity, prostitution, and drug abuse. Almost always the experience leaves psychological alienation from other people, deep emotional numbness and a horrifying series of flashbacks of those childhood experiences. As a result, many innocent victims suffer intensely.

To flee sexual immorality is to flee incest.

The forces that lead professing Christians in common with other Americans to commit acts of sexual deviancy vary with each person. These have been dealt with in other studies, with much helpful guidance now available. In this volume, my purpose is to simply call attention to the deflection from God's standards by many of His children and to encourage them to adopt a firm stance by voluntary self-discipline in this vulnerable area.

HONOR GOD WITH YOUR BODY

While Paul's first Christian response to immoral use of the body is to flee sexual immorality, the second response is to "*honor God with your body.*" In 1 Corinthians 6, Paul gives us three reasons for doing so: The body is (1) eternal, (2) the temple of the Holy Spirit, and (3) an instrument for Christ's use.

Paul writes: "By His power God raised the Lord from the dead, and He will raise us also" (1 Cor. 6:14). Our bodies will be raised from the dead someday. And enough of the old dust crumbled in our graves will be brought together to become the individuating principle of our souls for all eternity. We will know one another not by our spirits but by our bodies.

And we will know Jesus because He will be in His body. For Him, the Incarnation is eternal. One day He will return as He left at the Ascension—still in His body, the man Christ Jesus. An old hymn says, "I shall know Him, I shall know Him by the print of the nails in His hand." We need to honor God with our bodies because they are meant to be eternal. Although they will die, one day they will be raised again just as really as Christ's body was resurrected.

These human bodies also were created to be instruments for Christ to use (1 Cor. 6:15). We are encouraged to present our bodies to Him as living sacrifices (Rom. 12:1). I suggest that one practical way to make this sacrifice is to offer our five physical senses to Him. We must guard our eyes from seeing evil, our ears from hearing evil, our mouths from speaking evil, our nostrils from smelling evil, and our hands from touching evil. Occasionally, these physical senses need to be dedicated to Christ anew.

How can we honor God with our bodies? A helpful answer is found in Romans: "So then my brothers, you can see that we owe no duty to our sensual nature or to live life on the level of the instincts. Indeed, that way of living leads to certain spiritual death. But if on the other hand you cut the nerve of your instinctive actions by obeying the Spirit, you will live" (Rom. 8:12-13, PH).

How can we cut the nerve of our instinctive passions so that we can better obey the Holy Spirit? Do we take the vow of celibacy and live as though God made us without a sexual instinct? Some people indeed are called into such a life, and God has used them greatly. But for most of us, God expects us to live the way He created us—with sexual instincts.

But these are not to be fulfilled merely for physical gratification but for the spiritual purposes of God's creation. Ideally, sex is part of a spiritual union. Sex education classes which present only the biological aspects of sex leave out a major component—the spiritual—and this must be discovered as part of honoring Christ with our bodies. Sexuality must be taught in the context of values taught us by our Creator.

One inspiring illustration of honoring God with our bodies is to be seen in Charles Whiston, a long-time friend of mine who spent his last active years as a seminary professor teaching prayer to theological students and faculty members. Whiston is the only man I know who built a special room in his house for prayer. When my wife and I were overnight guests in his home in Santa Fe, New Mexico, we were invited to join the Whistons in their prayer chapel. Here the two pray together at the beginning and end of each day.

When later they moved to Carmel, where they built a retirement home, I asked him, "Were you able to keep a prayer room?"

"It was the first room we planned, and we built everything else around it," he said quietly.

Every night when the Whistons pray in their chapel, they intercede for a great host of people. They also repeat their marriage vows as part of their continuing relationship of love.

Charles Whiston wrote a book entitled *Pray: A Study of Distinctive Christian Prayer*, one of the most helpful contemporary books on prayer. It views the human body as a temple in which Jesus dwells through His Holy Spirit.

Writes Whiston about sex life: "It is sad indeed that sexual relationships are so utterly unrelated to God, the Creator and giver of sexual joys. The intimate relation of ecstatic joy in sexual union is a most holy gift of God. It is far more than a merely biological experience. Today both literature and films confront us frequently with a sordid degradation and perversion of sex, and we must oppose this trend."[24]

To ensure that even sexual union be under God's sovereignty, he suggests prayers to accompany it.

Before: "Lord Jesus Christ, we offer our bodies to Thee that by their union we may be instruments to bring each other Thy holy gift of joy and oneness. Here we are. Use us."[25]

After: "O Lord Jesus Christ, thanks be to Thee for the holy gift of ecstacy Thou hast given to us through our bodies."

Not every Christian will feel it appropriate to follow this suggestion. But how shall we respond to our world with its pervasive immorality and impurity? With the two powerful directions Paul gives us: Negatively—Let us flee sexual immorality! Positively—Let us honor God with our bodies.

EIGHT

THREATS TO MARRIAGE

When President Reagan's "Year of the Bible" ended in December 1983, he suggested that we begin a year of *practicing* Bible teaching in national life. Obeying God's Word, however, is more difficult than giving allegiance to it. That's because the Bible cuts across so many established ways of life in Western civilization. Certainly, this is true of marriage and the family.

In the 1950s when we were afraid of communist infiltration in the U.S. and were reading revolutionary Marxist books such as *Das Kapital*, Dr. Anton Pearson, professor of Old Testament at Bethel Seminary, used to tell students, "The most dangerous book in the world is the Bible!"

CALL FOR A COUNTERCULTURE

The Bible calls for a counterculture—urging people not to be conformed to this world, but to fulfill the ideals of God's kingdom. Nowhere is the contrast between ideals and reality seen more clearly than in Ephesians 5 and 6, a passage about ideals for the Christian family. It calls husbands and wives to stand against the tide. A simple reading of this text contradicts the practice of our times by giving three high ideals for the Christian marriage relationship:

1. *A well-ordered relationship*: "Submit to one another out of reverence for Christ. Wives, submit to your husbands as to the Lord. For the husband is the head of the wife as Christ is the head of the church, His body, of which He is the Saviour. Now as the church submits to Christ, so also wives should submit to their husbands in everything.

"Husbands, love your wives, just as Christ loved the church and gave Himself up for her to make her holy, cleansing her by the washing with water through the Word, and to present her to Himself as a radiant church, without stain or wrinkle or any other blemish, but holy and blameless. In this same way, husbands ought to love their wives as their own bodies. He who loves his wife, loves himself. After all, no one ever hated his own body, but he feeds and cares for it, just as Christ does the church—for we are members of His body" (Eph. 5:21-30).

The relationship between husband and wife has become one of the silent issues of the church because of the stridency of the feminist movement in the twentieth-century Western world. The feminist movement exists in other cultures, of course, but not in the same systematic, organized way.

Although the Equal Rights Amendment was not ratified, the rhetoric accompanying it has left a deep impression upon the soul of America. We are indebted to this rising consciousness of feminism for reminding us of sinful sexism long a part of our culture. But I do not think we need to rewrite the Scriptures or old church liturgies in terms of a neuter gender. I believe strong womanhood can relate meaningfully to God our Father just as she relates deeply to an earthly father. And I want to see Scriptures preserved in the way they were inspired by God Himself.

We are richer, however, for the new movement's reminders that God has used women in significant roles of religious leadership in the past. Many of our new Christian churches around the world would not exist were it not for dedicated, determined women. A greater role for women as leaders is possible in the future in all walks of life, including the church. All of this is to our good and makes us want to help remove the stigma of minority status from womankind.

However, we are not to reinterpret Scripture to make it mean something different. I've read many theological discussions about the word *kephala* in Ephesians 5:23, used to describe the husband as the *head* of the wife. Biblical scholars interpret and apply this word in such diverse ways that the average person becomes confused.

Since the New Testament was written in Koiné, not classical, Greek for the benefit of the average person, scholars who draw highly esoteric meanings from it do injustice to the Bible and the average layperson. Believing that the Bible is God's inspired Word and the final authority for faith and conduct, the average Christian should be able to use any adequate translation as a guide for his life.

For me, it is impossible to make this Ephesians passage say anything other than that the husband is intended to be head of the wife. A dozen different English translations express this.

In her recent book, *From Hierarchy to Equality*, an historical study of 1 Corinthians 11:2-16, Linda Mercadante related the changing status of women in society to traditional and nontraditional interpretations of Scripture, and sees value in both. She writes: "While in much of the earlier period hierarchy was a dominant thesis in the interpretation of this passage (1 Corinthians 11:1-16), in the modern period the stress has been shifted to the aspect of 'spiritual equality,' which was latent in the traditional position. In both the earlier and modern periods, however, the underlying intention has been the maintenance of the superordination/subordination theme. But the way of presenting this has clearly shifted in relation to culture's shifting values (e.g., from 'orderliness' and 'keeping one's place' to 'freedom' and 'fulfillment')."[1]

She anticipates that ongoing research will find new light from the Scriptures on this controversial subject. Certainly, it is true that the essential oneness of humankind is indicated in passages such as Galatians 3:28: "There is neither Jew nor Greek, slave nor free, male nor female, for you are all one in Christ Jesus"; but ethnic, social, or gender differences are not obliterated.

Indeed, the glory of the church is that it is comprised of a variety of people with different endowments, gifts, and functions—people who are brothers and sisters on the same level in the family of God. The church is not a melting pot in which all members are melded into a homogeneous mass but a mosaic in which individual differences complement one another to the glory of God.

Everybody brings his own bias to this passage about headship in Ephesians, and I bring my administrative one. For the twenty-eight years I served as president of Bethel College and Seminary, I gave direction to an increasingly complex organization of people on campus. I learned quickly both from theory and practice that two people can never be put in charge of the same organization with equal responsibility. It is then impossible for the organization to operate effectively. Assignments cannot be pinned down and accountability is diffused.

When Paul talks about headship, he simply is talking about final accountability in the home. Not authoritarian, arbitrary, capricious, or dictatorial domination over a wife, but final accountability in the marriage: that is the assignment to the husband.

The sensitive and delicate love relationship that Paul sees in an ideal Christian marriage is the opposite of what we have stereotyped as a chain of command. Such a military figure was not in Paul's mind. Nor is it a political figure in which an organizational bureaucrat hands down a command for an underling to obey unthinkingly.

Paul is talking about a husband who loves his wife as much as Christ loves His church and is willing to bend his own desires—to die if need be as Christ did—to help his wife become her own best self under God. Such leadership in the home will lead to consultation, input, and consensus in mutual decision-making.

Such a husband is the head in the sense that he has final accountability to God for the orderly conduct of life in the home according to biblical ideals. I believe that when a husband loves his wife this much—and my wife tells me this is so—it is not all that difficult for her to be submissive to him. But such an ideal of headship—final accountability—moves against the trend of our times. Nevertheless, such accountability is essential to a well-ordered relationship between a husband and a wife.

2. *Marriage is a lifelong relationship.* The Ephesians 5 passage is an application of the seventh commandment in Deuteronomy 5 and Jesus' interpretation in Matthew 5. It is helpful to read them in sequence.

"It has been said, 'Anyone who divorces his wife must give her a certificate of divorce.' But I tell you that anyone who divorces his wife, except for marital unfaithfulness, causes her to commit adultery, and anyone who marries a woman so divorced commits adultery" (Matt. 5:31-32).

"You shall not commit adultery" (Deut. 5:18).

'For this reason a man will leave his father and mother and will be united to his wife, and the two will become one flesh.' This is a profound mystery—but I am talking about Christ and the church. However, each one of you also must love his wife as he loves himself, and the wife must respect her husband" (Eph. 5:31-33).

This ideal too is quite different from the American way of life as indicated by a survey in *Better Homes and Gardens* magazine. Out of 200,000 responses to a questionnaire about the home and family, 80 percent reported that they believe the American family is in trouble. The major reasons listed were lack of religious foundations, inattentiveness to children, moral decay, economic concerns, and the understandable tensions of a two-career home. When asked if they considered divorce an appropriate response to marital difficulties, 71 percent said yes. When asked if divorce was acceptable if there were children, 61 percent still responded yes. A clear majority approved divorce as a way out at all costs.[2]

In *Megatrends*, John Naisbitt reports about the shift from the family to the individual as society's building block.[3] He concludes that more than a third of all children born in the 1970s will have spent part of their childhood living with a single parent. Doubtless, this will have a decisive effect on our nation.

Divorce now is so widespread in the U.S.—40 percent of all marriages ending in dissolution—that divorce is rampant among Christian families also. While the divorce rate among Christians is somewhat lower than the national average, it still is tragically high. It is another area in which Christian ideals often are shaped more by our culture than by our Bibles. Divorce also is a silent issue of the church.

Every church has enough divorced people among its congregation on Sunday to keep the pastor from preaching directly about it in order to avoid opening old wounds. As a result, a whole generation of young people is growing up without exposure to the lifelong ideals of Christian marriage.

This is not to say that divorce is the unpardonable sin anymore than that adultery is unpardonable. The forgiveness of sin made possible by Christ's atoning death can cover all defection from biblical norms. Nor is it to say that a divorced person cannot serve Christ effectively. Nor do we fail to empathize with brothers and sisters who have gone through the heart-wrenching experience of marital separation. Nor is it that the church should avoid opening its doors wide for special ministries to single parents.

It does mean, however, that we will stand with the Lord God of Israel and declare as in Malachi 2:16: "I hate divorce." If the church is silent on this subject, who will speak out? Fortunately, some of our best allies are people who have gone through divorce. From often-bitter, personal involvement, they're eager to counsel new generations of couples in love, before and after marriage vows, but especially before.

Somehow we need to break through the silence of the church by ministering in a loving and redemptive way to those who have experienced the heartache of divorce while at the same time holding a high biblical standard of lifelong marriage for new generations of young couples.

What are the major causes for the large-scale breakup of marriages in our time? Three can be singled out:

• *Incompatibility.* I remember my own heartache when a personal friend regretfully told me, "I know the New Testament teaching against divorce, but my psychiatrist counsels me to get a divorce from my wife, because of our incompatibility, and I have decided to follow his advice."

It seemed to him to be the only way out of a difficult situation. I could not judge him, both because I live in a glass house with my own failures and because I didn't live in his house with his problems. But if there is a clear difference between what the Word of God teaches and the advice of a counselor, whom are we to follow? It is easy for me to ask the question because of my own lifelong happiness with my marriage partner. But I know it is a terribly difficult question for people in the throes of marital problems.

The truth is that incompatibility can never be considered an adequate biblical reason for divorce. As long as two people live together, they will find some incompatibilities, and new ones will emerge through the years. A lifelong practice of working at resolving differences must be cultivated.

In his wedding sermon from a prison cell, Dietrich Bonhoeffer talks about the intention of God for marriage to be indissoluble. He teaches: "It is not your love which sustains the marriage but from now on the marriage sustains your love."[4]

A marriage vow must be worked out more seriously than it often is these days. The Elizabethan phrase, "I plight thee my troth," refers to trustworthiness, honesty, integrity, and faithfulness. Because of this, Dr. James Spickelmier, the Bethel campus pastor, taught students that when a young couple promises "for richer, for poorer, for better, for worse, in sickness and in health, until death do us part," it means that the marriage is for keeps.

When our youngest daughter was about to be married, we looked over some old wedding invitations we had received for help to compose a new one. We were taken aback by one from a promising couple who invited us to share their joy because "we know God has intended us for each other." God must have changed His mind because we remembered that within a year they had been divorced! They are no different from hosts of Christian couples today. One of America's residual problems left over from the '60s is the tentative spirit and lack of total commitment brought into marriage.

If we do not take God seriously, "Let your 'Yes' be 'Yes,' and your 'No' be 'No'," when we recite the marriage vow before our friends, pastors and official witnesses, when can we be trusted to keep our word? A vow—"till death do us part"—is meant to be kept as long as life shall last, not as long as love shall last.

Certainly, our vow is meant to be more long-lived than that indicated by the title of Zane Alexander's book, *Till Death Do Us Part or Something Else Comes Up.*[5] Sheer incompatibility, which often can be resolved in patience and love, must not be allowed to destroy a marriage. Once entered, marriage is to be a lifelong relationship, according to God's Word.

● *Infidelity.* This is a second cause for shipwreck of marriages. All major research reports on the sexual practice of Americans— among them Kinsey, Masters and Johnson, and Hite—agree that a large percentage of both husbands and wives are unfaithful and engage in extramarital relationships. Ironically, some couples stay together only by allowing sexual freedom to each other!

Tragically, unfaithfulness is a characteristic also of many Christian marriages and reflects another capitulation to accepted cultural practices. Two of my friends, both professionals in public service and active churchmen—one Baptist and the other Roman Catholic—appeared in prominent news stories in our local paper. One had been arrested leaving a house of prostitution and the other was apprehended inside. Both pleaded guilty and suffered enormous consequences in their public life. They were professing Christians but unfaithful marriage partners.

During the recent past, two highly visible evangelical leaders acknowledged to me their sexual infidelity. Happily, both of them had experienced forgiveness and restoration to their partners in an inspiring new relationship with Christ.

It is especially heartbreaking to hear of pastors who prove untrue to their wives. One evangelical pastor, to my knowledge, actually seduced a dozen different women in his congregation and continued preaching to them on Sundays. None of them knew about the others, nor did his wife. Fortunately, he dropped out of the ministry. I believe he also resolved his deep inner problems. But if moral lapses occur in the parsonage, the congregation no longer has an adequate model for the biblical ideal of marriage. Little wonder that the homes of the congregation begin to reflect the lowered standards of the world.

If a biblical basis exists for divorce, unfaithfulness may be it. This is how I understand Matthew 5. Scholars disagree about this interpretation. But, of course, divorce need not necessarily follow unfaithfulness. Forgiveness, restoration of the marriage, and rebuilding of love still are possible. In fact, one of the most strategic areas of ministry open to churches today is to help renew marriages flawed by infidelity and thus meet one of the deep spiritual needs of many members. Recently, I have seen the rebuilding of marriage demonstrated beautifully in the experience of a Christian couple who are among our warm friends. Their marriage was in jeopardy because of the adultery of the husband. But in their darkest hour, both experienced a new commitment to God as well as a new love for one another. Today they are radiantly happy with Christ as the very center of their new life. Sometimes a spouse may need a new partner. But it can be the same one—only renewed through forgiveness and restoration.

● *Alternative sexual lifestyles.* A third serious threat to the biblical concept of marriage—lifelong monogamy—is found in the easy acceptance of alternative sexual lifestyles (see chapter 7 for a fuller discussion). These include what television host Phil Donahue calls free-form marriages. As an example, on a national telecast he interviewed two men and one woman living together in what they felt was a normal relationship.

The contemporary nonmarriage is another variant in which a couple simply lives together as long as it is convenient. The most recent U.S. census lists more than 1.9 million persons living as couples without the benefit of marriage. Most relationships are less permanent than the old common-law marriages recognized by law but probably more permanent than the "shacking up" of the '70s. In all instances, however, they are less than the biblical ideal for a marriage commitment and are beset by a myriad of personal, legal, social, and professional problems.

Swinging couples and wife swapping are still in vogue, especially among the Yuppies (young urban professionals). But it is still a violation of one of God's most fundamental rules for living—lifelong faithfulness to one partner.

Another alternative to conventional marriage is the homosexual relationship discussed at length in chapter 7. As gays have come out of the closet and homosexuality has become an accepted variant of human sexuality, more and more marriage partners are leaving their heterosexual spouses to live openly with another person of their own sex.

I believe that the Christian can discover from God's Word that God is sufficient even for the homosexual. God will either help the person to become heterosexual or keep him or her from practicing homosexuality in spite of tendencies.[6] Only as God is allowed to work in these ways will this threat to traditional marriage be diminished.

All three of these causes for marital failure—incompatibility, infidelity, and alternative sexual lifestyles—are so easily accepted by our culture that the church must take a more public stand if its members are to take seriously the biblical ideal of marriage as a lifelong partnership under God.

3. *Christian marriage is to be a nurturing relationship:* "Children, obey your parents in the Lord, for this is right. 'Honor your father and mother'—which is the first commandment with a promise—'that it may go well with you and that you may enjoy long life on the earth.' Fathers, do not exasperate your children; instead, bring them up in the training and instruction of the Lord" (Eph. 6:1-4).

Christian nurture is *implicit* in the loving relationship of a husband and wife and *explicit* in the training relationship of a parent and child. A biblical family's cohesiveness runs counter to the fragmental, spasmodic, and hurried contacts many modern parents have with their children.

Often for understandable reasons, a parent's influence upon a child is broken and incomplete. Alienation within the family characterizes altogether too many homes and destroys family life.

I remembered how deeply moved I was when at a spiritual life retreat I asked a group of seminarians to identify the most Christlike person in their lives. One senior responded immediately, "My father." It is not difficult to obey such a parent.

Parental nurture, like organizational accountability, includes praisings as well as reprimands, perhaps in the ratio of ten to one. It is much easier to scold than to compliment, but one scolding has more impact when preceded by ten compliments. When the artist Ben West was asked, "What made you become such a great artist?" he replied simply, "The smile of my mother." As in the case of a plant, nurture is not only in pruning but in watering.

Lifelong nurturing also is intended in the love relationship between a husband and wife. Ideally, they become soul friends to one another, sharing their highest and lowest moments together with God. Like England's Keswick Convention for spiritual pilgrims, their home becomes a place to repair the damage to the soul caused by the wear and tear of life. A joyous spontaneity exists in their marriage which makes each day a new adventure.

My wife, Nancy, and I have discovered a deep melding of our own hearts as we begin each day—while still in bed—reading

God's Word and classical books of Christian devotion. Together we discuss the day ahead and then pray for His direction in the details of that day. A couple can minister to each other in many ways in the name of the Lord and thus strengthen their marriage bond. Christian nurture is expanded to include the parents as well as the children and each becomes a minister to the others. The example of the parents becomes a nurturing model to the children.

The three emphases of Ephesians 5—that a Christian marriage relationship is meant to be well-ordered, lifelong, and nurturing— is a bulwarking word from God for the tottering homes of America.

NINE

THE CHALLENGE TO VOLUNTARY SELF-DISCIPLINE

For the Christian, *voluntary* self-discipline is a free response of love to the lordship of Christ in his life. Each day we need to say a big no to self in order to keep saying a big yes to Christ.

When we obey earthly rules and regulations, we must practice self-discipline to measure up. That is, even when a traffic cop is not in sight and we are tempted to exceed the speed limit, we discipline ourselves to conform. However, when I speak of *voluntary* self-discipline for the Christian, I mean he imposes upon himself a pattern of behavior because he believes it is the best way to live. With his free will—not because of laws or other outside restrictions—he chooses to carry out the ideal he has established.

Not all devout Christians agree with me about the areas which call for self-denial or about the issues discussed in this book. I certainly do not suggest a universal code of behavior for all Christians in all cultures at all times. I do not even presume to think that any evangelical proscription of behavior ought to be enforced on a broad scale in our culture.

I do believe that the issues I have raised are sufficiently serious to justify a response by Christians in America today to voluntarily saying no to their culture—and to themselves.

LAWS GOVERNING CHRISTIAN BEHAVIOR

There are at least three levels of law that govern Christian behavior and require obedience.

The first is *divine law*, such as the unchanging Ten Commandments of Exodus 20. Stealing, adultery, lying, and murdering always are wrong and subject to God's penalties.

The second is *civil law*. In Romans 13:1-7 and 1 Peter 2:11-17, the Christian is told that his testimony as a believer requires obedience to his government's statutes, except when they conflict with God's Law (Acts 5:29).

The third is *community law*, in which groups of people agree to come under common regulations to live orderly and comfortably together (Acts 15:29). In my experience such community groups have included service clubs with their attendance stipulations, college accrediting associations with their performance stipulations, and Christian college communities with their lifestyle stipulations.

Each set of laws becomes mandatory for us: the divine laws because of our creation by God, the civil laws because of our citizenship, and the community laws because of our membership in a specific group. Not every action prohibited by civil or community law is inherently evil—sprinkling lawns on a day when sprinkling is banned, driving 40 mph in a 35 mph zone, or parking overtime at a meter. But because such actions have adverse effects upon community life, they are part of the larger network of regulations to which we voluntarily give obedience.

SAYING NO TO GAIN THE BEST

At the level of self-discipline, individuals committed to Christ may choose to reject practices not inherently evil in order to excel as Christians. This is like a piano pupil who may say no to a baseball game in order to practice and one day excel as a pianist. Or a basketball player who may say no to a night out with friends in order to rest and perhaps excel in the next day's game. Or a model who may say no to a dessert in order to remain trim and excel in her profession. So the Christian, besides saying no to evil, often must say no to what is good in his or her quest for the best.

This is the point of Paul's metaphors in 2 Timothy 2, likening the Christian to a soldier refusing civilian entanglements, to an athlete abiding by the rules, and to a farmer toiling diligently in the fields. These prototypes illustrate that a disciplined life requires the rejection of even good things: enabling the soldier to win the battle, the athlete to win the contest, and the farmer to reap the harvest.

Bishop Stephen Neill encouraged Christians not to be afraid of emphasizing the role of self-discipline in their lives, insisting it was complementary to spontaneity and immediate inspiration. "It is by endlessly repeated decisions in relation to trivial things that the general direction of our lives is in the end determined," he said. "The realm of the exceedingly ordinary is also the realm of the Holy."[1]

This was emphasized for college students by Dr. W. Robert Smith, professor of philosophy at Bethel College. He encouraged students to deny themselves a Coke occasionally when they were about to buy one, just for the sake of practicing self-denial. His point was that if we haven't learned to say no to self in little things, we will not be able to say no to self in big things.

Such discipline is characteristic of the "disciple of Christ," the term used more than 250 times in the New Testament to refer to the Christian. Discipline and discipleship are concepts which belong together. Christian discipleship is the life of surrender to Christ as Lord, resulting in eagerness to learn from Him, willingness to obey Him, and readiness to serve Him—all to the point of total expendability.

Voluntary self-discipline is not arbitrary legalistic bondage or code-ethics but rather a spontaneous inner response of love to the sanctifying work of the Holy Spirit. One of the fruits of His presence is self-control (Gal. 5:22), or self-discipline, intended to help us achieve the ultimate goal of discipleship—such a complete union with Christ that His life is lived through ours.

CRUCIFIXION AND THE RISEN LIFE

In this process, an alternating tension exists between Christ's call to a life of self-denial—saying no to self—and to the abundant life—saying yes to Christ. Both self-renunciation and self-fulfillment are meant to be simultaneous experiences in our spiritual growth. Self-discipline, in the biblical sense, is the key to the exchanged life.

This exchange is symbolized in the Scriptures by the crucified and the risen life. Both Jesus and Paul call us to these experiences. There is a frequent call to the Cross in the New Testament:

"Anyone who does not take his cross and follow Me is not worthy of Me" (Matt. 10:38).

"If anyone would come after Me, he must deny himself and take up his cross and follow Me" (Matt. 16:24; Mark 8:34).

"Those who belong to Christ Jesus have crucified the sinful nature with its passions and desires" (Gal. 5:24).

"For you died, and your life is now hidden with Christ in God" (Col. 3:3).

"For we know that our old self was crucified with Him so that the body of sin might be rendered powerless" (Rom. 6:6).

Concomitantly, for the Apostle Paul, coresurrection—with Christ—accompanied cocrucifixion. Death to self meant a rich entrance into a new life.

"I have been crucified with Christ and I no longer live, but Christ lives in me. The life I live in the body, I live by faith in the Son of God, who loved me and gave Himself for me" (Gal. 2:20).

"And He died for all, that those who live should no longer live for themselves but for Him who died for them and was raised again" (2 Cor. 5:15).

"We always carry around in our body the death of Jesus, so that the life of Jesus may also be revealed in our body" (2 Cor. 4:10).

"In the same way, count yourselves dead to sin but alive to God in Christ Jesus" (Rom. 6:11).

To read these antithetical calls—to die and to come alive—as the key to self-discipline is to sense that the disciple's self-renunciation can lead gloriously to his self-fulfillment. This inner spiritual experience takes place deep within us—far below the level of waking consciousness. This is where the self is fundamentally constituted. This level is the arena of natural instincts—drives, urges, needs, or triggers of action—those forces inherited from our ancestors' genes and chromosomes which make us behave as we do. They are what Paul calls the flesh.

George B. Cutten, then president of Colgate University, defined an instinct as "an insistent but unlearned activity toward originally unrecognized ends, which is common to the species, and the consummation of which may be modified by experience."[2] Cutten's conclusion that the instinct's activity is modifiable coincides with the New Testament teaching about conversion. The Holy Spirit can change a person so radically in his interior life that he is born all over again.

Regeneration takes place in the arena of the instincts and is a secret, mystical soul experience, however apparent the outward change—conversion—may be. Just how many instincts we have isn't agreed on; the number depends upon the perspective of the psychologist delving into them. McDougal lists 12; James, 40; and Watson, 100. Freud reduced them to one!

However delineated, they include such drives as hunger, sexual desire, love, security, protectiveness, acquisitiveness, curiosity, gregariousness, fear, anger, and creativity. At the level of instincts, man was fundamentally flawed in the Fall. When the holy God drove sinful Adam from the Garden and left him, Adam's life's unifying center was taken away. Instinctive drives, once directed in an orderly way toward the divine center, lost their spiritual cohesion, and man was left a frustrated soul.

Thus Paul cried out, "I do not understand what I do. For what I want to do I do not do, but what I hate I do" (Rom. 7:15). Augustine prayed, "O God, we were meant for Thee and we will never rest until we rest in Thee."

Our deep, inner, instinctive life is like the field of magnetism created when a magnet is brought under a sheet of paper holding iron filings. No matter how chaotic a jumble they lay in when the magnet approaches, the filings leap into place—neat, symmetrical, and beautiful. So it is with the inner chaos of a life under the impact of sin. When Christ is allowed to move into its center, all basic drives are restructured in an orderly relationship around Him.

Life, then, is marked by a peace that passes understanding. The Greek root *irene* means not only "peace" but "rope"—like threads of hemp in a cluster on a floor picked up and woven together neatly and symmetrically into a strong cord. So God reorients the basic instincts fragmented by sin and infuses them with His Spirit.

Paul commends this basic revolution in instinctive behavior: "So then, my brothers, you can see that we owe no duty to our sensual nature, or to live life on the level of the instincts. Indeed that way of living leads to certain spiritual death. But if on the other hand you cut the nerve of your instinctive actions by obeying the Spirit, you are on your way to real living" (Rom. 8:12-13, PH).

Cutting the nerve of our instinctive actions to put us on the road to real living includes both self-renunciation and self-fulfillment. How does the Holy Spirit achieve this in us? By suppressing our instincts and making us live as if we didn't have them? By denying our hunger instincts, for example, and making us endure a long fast? By denying our sex drives and calling us to celibacy? By denying our gregarious natures and sending us into a hermitage?

Of course, God sometimes leads people into all of these experiences to achieve some high spiritual end. But these are special callings. Normally, God expects us to live according to the way He created us. He made us with all our instincts. These are to be directed toward Christ at the center of our lives and toward His purpose and His glory—not just toward our sensual satisfaction. The chief end of man, indeed, is to glorify God and enjoy Him forever.

If our instinctive responses are only self-centered, we become victims of all the aberrations that L.E. Maxwell describes in his book *Born Crucified* as the hyphenated self-sins: self-confidence, self-esteem, self-saving, self-pity, self-defense, self-vindication, self-seeking, self-centeredness, self-inspection, self-accusation, self-pleasing, self-choosing, self-assertiveness, self-boasting, self-expressing, self-indulgence, self-satisfaction, self-admiration, self-congratulation, self-justification, self-righteousness, self-complacency, self-glory, self-love—and selfishness, though not hyphenated.[3]

What a tangled life results when instinctive behavior responds to all of these contradictory impulses in life.

My view of the crucified Christian life is that it is the life so under the control of the Holy Spirit that all its basic drives are redirected from mere self-gratification to the purposes of Christ and His kingdom. Instincts normally are not meant to be throttled by rigorous asceticism, but to be redirected by God's power toward Christ, the divine center of our inner life. They are to be recognized as a gift from our Creator and are not to be used self-indulgently.

SELF-DISCIPLINE UNDER THE SPIRIT

We are not to frustrate these inner urges by self-flagellation, but instead, by self-discipline under the Holy Spirit's control, we are to allow our instincts to find their highest expression in our relationship to Christ. Then the response center of life—that subconscious level of instinctive behavior—will be shifted from self to the Holy Spirit.

Our instinct for food illustrates this. Paul's decription of the Cretans, who made gods of their bellies, fits our social life today. Eating and drinking is such a part of our celebrations that we feel forced to participate whether or not we need food. Even in our everyday life, we've placed a central focus on food.

In chapter 6, I indicated that because of undisciplined eating habits a third of Americans are too heavy. Obesity has become one of our most serious national health problems. However, when this basic instinct is redirected from purely physical gratification to the spiritual purposes of Christ for our bodies, it is possible to eat and drink to the glory of God (1 Cor. 10:31). Our food intake will be aimed at keeping our bodies fit temples of the Holy Spirit and keen instruments for His use. Our voluntary acts of self-discipline reflect a deeper control by the Spirit of God in our inner instinctive behavior.

Similarly, the sex drive—so exploited in America today—can be brought under this reorienting power of the Holy Spirit. Then it no longer expresses itself for only physical gratification in a *Playboy*-saturated culture. It is expressed for God's primary purposes of loving companionship and for continuing the human family. The God to whom we've given our highest love so motivates us in our human love relationships that the most intimate physical experiences of marriage are sanctified by His presence. Two who have been made one seek together to serve Him more effectively.

Another urge—the drive for social approval—also illustrates this basic supernatural shift in our inner focus. The desire to be well thought of by others leads to many compromises. Even enslave ment to the changing fashions of the day reflects an instinctive reluctance to be out of line with others.

The Holy Spirit can redirect this force so that we seek the approval of Christ and His followers. His "well done, thou good and faithful servant" becomes more important to us than the plaudits of a fickle crowd. Then we discover the genuine delight of the old mystics who declared, "I can do anything I please—because I please to do only that which glorifies God."

When we surrender to Christ's love, we don't suppress our essential nature. We simply allow the Holy Spirit to refocus it.

Bishop Neill insists that this new focus is one of the most important characteristics of the twentieth-century Christian saint. In his book *Christian Holiness,* he describes three such characteristics—an ability to live at home in a world that cannot be seen, an endless wellspring of contagious joy, and an integration of everything in life under the lordship of Christ.[4]

A purposeful surrender of exterior things—money, homes, automobiles, careers, families—to Christ as Lord is but the outward expression of a profound inward change that God effects at a subconscious level. What formerly were self-centered forces now find their most creative fulfillment in Christ. What began as death to self has become new life in Christ.

Ruth Paxton, in her volume *Life on the Highest Plane,* looked upon this experience as the maturing of the believer. "The spiritual man," she wrote, "is the man who has made the will of Jesus Christ the center and circumference of his life . . . who acknowledges that he has no life apart from Christ and takes the Lord Jesus for everything in his inner life, his environment and his service . . . who has crowned Christ Lord and placed his life completely under the control of his Master."[5]

Nowhere in the New Testament is the cost of discipleship more powerfully portrayed than in Luke 14. Three times Jesus declares that a person cannot be His disciple without dying to self. A disciple must "hate" his loved ones (v. 26), shoulder his cross (v. 27), and give up all he possesses (v. 33). The cost of discipleship is sobering in terms of personal relationships, personal ambitions, and personal posssessions. However, as disciples we do not abandon these things. We continue to have beloved relatives, cherished ambitions, and possessions. But we have died to them as ends in themselves or as ways to fulfill self-centered instincts.

All continue to be significant in our lives now controlled by the Holy Spirit, but only as they relate to Christ and His lordship. This fundamental outlook arises from the inner transformation of our basic drives to reflect a self-discipline—self control—which is a fruit of the Holy Spirit. It is internalized self-restraint.

This inner transformation enables us to say no to ourselves and no to our culture. Such self-discipline is desperately needed in our time by people both American and Christian. Our call is to a life which begins at the cross.

In *The Fellowship of the Saints,* Thomas Kepler describes 127 of the writing saints in church history as radiant persons, "living with a joyous, radiant, light-hearted freedom because life is totally dependent on God."[6]

Radiance is an indefinable quality of soul, but it is the ultimate mark of Christ's union with us and ours with Him.

One visitor to Canaan in Darmstadt, Germany described the merry Sisters of Mary there by saying, "They twinkle a lot!" All of these people lived disciplined lives in which they discovered that saying yes to Christ's values eclipsed saying no to cultural pressures. As a result, they were contagiously happy.

I knew just such a saint. His name was Harold Lidbom, and for more than a dozen years, he was the business manager on my administrative team at Bethel College and Seminary. I was alternately inspired and rebuked as I watched him give himself expendably in ministry to others. It didn't make any difference what the need was—a new family needing a guide to look for homes for sale, a neighbor on vacation needing a house-watcher, a widow needing her snow shoveled, a hospitalized acquaintance needing encouragement, a friend needing help with his car, a lonely person needing a smile of appreciation, a hungry student needing a meal, a church task needing a volunteer to carry it out— Harold was there. And he was there cheerfully, optimistically, eagerly. We lived in the same block as Harold, and through the years every member of my family was on the receiving end of his thoughtful acts—telephone calls, visits, gifts, meals, household errands, and many other simple acts of thoughtfulness. What he did so compassionately for others during a lifetime he did lovingly for Gertrude, his wife, when in her later years she became helpless and unable to care for herself. Harold's no to self went far beyond moral and ethical issues to include the whole of life.

We were close enough to observe Harold as he constantly said no to his own plans, personal comfort, and need for rest in order to say yes to Christ and to others in His name. He celebrated life with others because of his commitment to the Lord and in the process he was deeply loved by everyone. He concluded his career early at Bethel in order to give his last years as a volunteer worker on a mission field in Ethiopia, still saying no to the easy way in order to give himself more fully to Christ.

After I observed Harold, the concept of voluntary self-discipline was no longer a theory for me. He demonstrated that indeed it is possible to deny basic instinctive impulses in order to give oneself totally to Christ and His people.

I thank God for Harold Lidbom. My own life has been deeply enriched as through him I have seen the fulfillment of Christ's promise, "Whoever loses his life for My sake will find it" (Matt. 10:39).

THE SPIRITUAL TRADITION OF SELF-DISCIPLINE

The quest for disciplined Christian living is as old as the church itself. Discipline was a prominent theme in the literature of the writing saints. To be sure, their understanding of it differed and at times their application faltered. However varied the personalities of the old Christian mystics—St. Ignatius with his propensity for military order, Bernard of Clairvaux with his contagious love for God, Francis of Assisi with his austere life in the pigpen—all wrote about the mortification of both flesh and spirit.

MORTIFICATION DEFINED

Mortification is a word that appears in both the Old Testament and New Testament and, as defined by Margaret Miles, refers to "the activity of dying to one's compulsive pursuit of lesser goods in order to pursue with undiluted energy and affection relationships to God, the ultimate good of the whole human being."[1]

Mortification was a common word in the desert and in monasteries as an outgrowth of Paul's figurative use of it in the Scriptures. Basically, mortification meant death to the self-life apart from Christ. Like many religious practices, mortification often was carried to extreme physical hardship. For some medieval saints, it included hairshirts, beds of spikes, and flagellation. For others, it was a gentler conditioning of the body. Sometimes the form lived on long after the spirit had been lost. The heavy emphasis grew out of a philosophic dualism which separated the body from the spirit and viewed the flesh as inherently sinful, needing punishment.

For others, mortification was probably an addiction to an ascetic practice, inducing an exhilarating chemical response of well-being similar to that which modern joggers experience. For still others, mortification was a frank recognition of sinful propensities and the need for contrite humbling before God.

At its highest, mortification referred to disciplines growing out of vigorous inner self-restraint prompted by the Holy Spirit. Just as the disciples learned in Gethsemane that the spirit may be willing but the body weak (Mark 14:38), so Christian saints in all ages have faced a dichotomy between the spirit's good intentions and the body's basic instincts. The ultimate purpose of mortification was not the restriction of the body but the enlargement of the soul in its love for God.

TRY CLASSICAL DEVOTIONAL READING
The modern pilgrim can dip down into almost any age of church history and discover this holy desire for life under discipline. This is where the reading of classical devotional literature is helpful. A cumulative impact results from reading successively the yearnings of God's great souls. One can begin with Augustine in the patristic period. Among his confessions he wrote, "I hesitate to take that step that would make me die to death and live to life. I was too accustomed to the worst in me and too unaccustomed to the better. . . . I was held back by trifling nonsense—old loves that pluck softly at the robe of my flesh and murmured, 'Are you going to send us away, forever and forever? It means you will never be allowed to do this and that again.' What were they suggesting by 'this and that?' My God, let Your mercy keep the soul of Your servant from such actions."[2]

Augustine's full conversion came when he turned to God's Word and responded to Paul's counsel, "Let us behave decently, as in the daytime, not in orgies and drunkenness, not in sexual immorality and debauchery, not in dissension and jealousy. Rather, clothe yourselves with the Lord Jesus Christ, and do not think about how to gratify the desires of the sinful nature" (Rom. 13:13-14).

Later on in the Dark Ages, Benedict of Nursia stressed this aspect of the Christian life, saying, "Our hearts must, therefore, be ready to do battle under the biddings of the holy obedience; and let us ask the Lord that He supply by the help of His grace what is impossible to us by nature."

Benedict also talked about sensual discoveries—pleasurable physical experiences still being sought by new generations of Christians—saying, "We must therefore guard against all evil desires because death has his station near the entrance of pleasure."[2]

In the golden age of mysticism, Thomas a Kempis found the secret of discipleship in the imitation of Christ and wrote what author Thomas Elwell terms "religion's second bestseller." In it, a Kempis confesses his need for Christ to subdue his passions:

> My problem is this:
>   I feel my senses contradicting my mind,
>   Sin leading me captive to my senses;
>   I simply cannot resist my passions
>   Unless Your holy grace captures my heart.
> I need Your grace, O Lord,
>   and I need it in large supply
>   so that I will overcome my nature,
>   prone to evil from youth.
> Adam, the first person, passed on corruption,
>   and we all suffer the penalty;
>   Nature, which You make perfectly, now
>   misleads us,
>   The proof of which is, left to itself,
>   it migrates to evil and lower things.
> The small spark of good still in us
>   lies hidden in the ashes.
> This is natural reason, cradled in darkness,
>   yet capable of discerning right from wrong,
>   but incapable of doing what it knows,
>   and no longer enjoying the full light of truth
>   or soundness in its affections.[4]

In the sixteenth century, we meet Lawrence Scupoli, whose *Spiritual Combat* became one of the most influential classics in Catholic spirituality. Frances de Sales carried a copy for eighteen years and read from it daily. Scupoli insists that the spiritual life does not consist of external practices: "It actually consists in knowing the greatness and goodness of God, together with a true sense of our own weakness and evil, in loving God and hating ourselves, in humbing ourselves not only before Him, but for His sake, before all men, in renouncing entirely our own will in order to follow His. It consists, finally, in doing all of this solely for the glory of His holy name, for only one purpose—to please Him; for only one motive—that He should be loved and served by all His creatures."[5]

When Scupoli discussed spiritual combat, he distinguished carefully between the flesh and spirit: "For whoever has the courage to conquer his passions, to subdue his appetites and repulse even the least motions of his will, performs an action more meritorious in the sight of God than if, without this, he should tear his flesh with the sharpest disciplines, fast with greater austerity than the Ancient Fathers of the Desert, or convert multitudes of sinners."[6]

Richard Baxter appeared on the scene in seventeenth-century England with one of the most powerful books of that period, *The Reformed Pastor*. Although his concern was for the spiritual renewal of pastors, he left a deep impact upon the whole church. When he urges spiritual leaders to exercise oversight of themselves, he writes:

"Take heed to yourself, for you have a depraved nature. Your sinful inclinations are like those of everyone else. However much we may preach against sin, it still dwells in us. One degree of sin prepares the heart for another, and one sin inclines the mind to yet another. As a spark is the beginning of the flame, and as a minor disease may lead to one more serious, so there is an aversion to God within us, there is a strangeness that is irrational and unruly.

"Since, then, there are so many traitors in our hearts, is it not time for us to take heed? How easily our passions and inordinate desires are kindled by perverting our judgments or abating our resolution, cooling our zeal, and dulling our diligence. . . . It is vital for us, then, to realize how weak we are. Then we will be careful with the dieting and exercise of our souls."[7]

Following Baxter, William Law became a writing prophet to eighteenth-century England through his greatest work, *A Serious and Devout Call to a Holy Life*. In it he traces the Christian's inner struggle, saying:

> Our souls may receive an infinite hurt, and be rendered incapable of all virtue, merely by the use of innocent and lawful things. What is more innocent than rest and retirement? And yet what more dangerous than sloth and idleness? What is more lawful than eating and drinking? And yet what more destructive of all virtue . . . than sensuality and indulgence? How lawful and praiseworthy is care of a family? And yet how certainly are many people rendered incapable of all virtue by a worldly and solicitous temper. How it is for want of religious exercises in the use of these innocent and lawful things, that religion cannot get possession of our hearts? And it is the right and prudent management of ourselves, as to these things, that all the art of holy living chiefly consists."[8]

A century later Emily Herman produced her famous work, *Creative Prayer,* in which she continued the centuries-long conversation about self-discipline. "Our habitual misuse of words," she wrote, "has led us to imagine that Christian freedom consists in the moment, and we protest against anything that would put fetters upon this liberty . . . True spontaneousness is the fruit of discipline. It is the artist who has mastered the technique of his art most perfectly who can best respond to the vision and inspiration of the moment."[9]

More than a century ago the Keswick Convention was born in England and began to unfold the biblical doctrine of sanctification by faith. It became one of the most powerful renewal movements in Great Britain and continues its influence to this day. Evans Hopkins, one of Keswick's founders, preached and wrote that victory over sin is not to be found in eradication or suppression but in counteraction. He referred to the lifting influence of the Holy Spirit in counteracting sin's downward pull upon the inner life.

"The criterion of the highest and perfect moral state," he wrote, "is pleasure—when good acts are not only done but when we take pleasure in doing them. . . . We have, then, two stages of experience, both included in the life of a Christian—the one being animated chiefly by a sense of right, the other by the power of love. We may illustrate the two stages by two concentric circles—the outer circle representing the duty-life, and the inner circle the love-life. We may be within the first and yet not within the second; but it is impossible to be in the inner circle and not be in the outer circle also. So if we are 'dwelling in love,' we shall know what it is to do the right for its own sake as well as from inclination. But it is not difficult to see which of the two conditions is the true life of liberty."[10]

When we get to our own century, A.W. Tozer, the mystic of the Christian and Missionary Alliance, is a representative voice. He writes: "Let a man become enamored of Eternal Wisdom and set his heart to win her, he takes on himself a full-time, all-engaging pursuit. Thereafter, his whole life will be filled with seekings and findings, self-repudiations, tough disciplines, and daily dyings as he is being crucified unto the world and the world unto him. . . . It is the believer's own cross by means of which the cross of Christ is made effective in slaying his evil nature and setting him free from its power. . . . The Christian can refuse to take up his cross or . . . take it up and start for the dark hill. The difference between great sainthood and spiritual mediocrity depends upon which choice he makes."[11]

Always, however, the dark hill leads to the open grave and to the new life in Christ. Thus, Gordon Wakefield properly reminds us that Christian spirituality "is not simply for the interior life or the inward person, but as much for the body as the soul, and is directed to the implementation of both the commandments of Christ, to love God and our neighbor. Indeed our love, like God's, should extend to the whole creation."[12]

LET'S BE RADIANT REFLECTORS
Whatever God may be pleased to do for us in our times of spiritual retreat and inner reflection is not meant for purely ecstatic personal enjoyment. It is meant to make us

more radiant reflectors of His glory among our friends and sharper instruments for His use in our world. Even among the ancients, the highways of life led to the monastery, and intercessory prayer for the world came from the hermitage. At their highest, neither were so in touch with God that they were out of touch with His world.

My favorite character apart from Christ in the New Testament is John the Baptist. Perhaps this is because of the focus of his life: "He must become greater; I must become less" (John 3:30). Principal Denny of Scotland exuded the same spirit as he taught young men for the ministry, "Remember that you cannot at the same time show that Christ is wonderful—and you are clever." So much progress did John make toward Christlikeness that one day the friends who grew up with him in the wilderness came with a question. They knew him like an open book, but they asked, "Tell us who you really are, Elijah? A prophet come to life? But some asked, "Are you the Messiah?" What a wonderful mistake to make, to think that a friend we know could possibly be the Christ!

Jesus praised John for his steadfastness and fidelity under persecution. Just before he was beheaded by the angry Herod, against whose sins he had spoken fearlessly, John was languishing in jail, but yet was faithful. People could still see the Messiah in him. Our response to being treated unfairly may, indeed, be the greatest test of our Christlikeness. My predecesor at Bethel, Dr. Henry Wingblade, used to say that Christian personality is hidden deep inside of us. It is unseen like the soup carried in a tureen high over a waiter's head. No one knows what's inside—unless the waiter is bumped and he trips! Just so, people don't know what's inside of us until we've been bumped. But if Christ is living inside, what spills out is the fruit of the Spirit.

How preeminent is Christ in our lives? Well, what do the people who know us best—our spouse or children or brothers and sisters—think? And when we've been discriminated against in life, how much like Jesus are our reactions? It is from John the Baptist that I have learned to ask those two questions of myself repeatedly.

These are the questions that bring me back to the church mystics and their quest for Christian perfection—that is, a perfection of love for Christ. These voices of the past still call us to say no to ourselves and yes to our Lord.

ELEVEN

RESOURCES FOR SELF-DISCIPLINE

It is possible to say a big no to the world when we say a big yes to Christ. The personal conflict between the darkness of Satan's world and the light of Christ's kingdom is sketched graphically by John. It is climaxed with this exhortation:

> Do not love the world or anything in the world. If anyone loves the world, the love of the Father is not in him. For everything in the world—the cravings of sinful man, the lust of his eyes, and the boasting of what he has and does—comes not from the Father but from the world. The world and its desires pass away, but the man who does the will of God lives forever (1 John 2:15-17)

LOVING GOD

It was clear to John that it is impossible to love both the world and the Father at the same time. These loves are mutually exclusive. But love for the Father enables us to resist the inner urges of sinful man in order to carry out the will of God for us. Thus, it is our love for God that becomes the greatest motivational power, enabling us to say no to the enervating forces of our culture.

The cravings listed by John are universal. They tripped up Eve in the Garden. And they were the basis on which Satan sought to gain mastery over Jesus on the Mount of Temptation. All seven of the deadly sins feared by the early Christian saints issue from those cravings—pride, envy, anger, sloth, avarice, gluttony, and lust. They are the inner urges of the heart marked, as Jesus described it, by "evil thoughts, murder, adultery, sexual immorality, theft, false testimony, slander" (Matt. 15:19). This dark, unredeemed inner world can feed a love relationship with the forces of hell. Or it can be overcome by love for God which strengthens our resistance to the devil.

It was Bernard of Clairvaux who 900 years ago exemplified love for God in such a dynamic way that his persuasive power is still felt in our world. One of scores of his writings, *The Love of God,* has emerged as a timeless classic of Christian devotion. And in evangelical churches all over the world, we still sing the prayer that concludes his hymn, "O Sacred Head, Now Wounded":

> *O make me thine forever;*
> *And should I fainting be,*
> *Lord, let me never, never*
> *Outlive my love to Thee.*

Bernard's magnum opus may have been his eighty-six sermons on the Song of Songs as a cycle of love songs between Christ and His bride. The whole church has been enriched by Bernard's teaching about the four degrees of love. To him, they moved in an ascending order of importance:

first degree—love of man for man's sake;
second degree—love of God for man's sake;
third degree—love of God for God's sake;
fourth degree—love of man for God's sake.[1]

To Bernard, the highest level of love was to love man whom God created because through him the purposes of God would be fulfilled. This is self-esteem at its best, sublimated to the sovereignty and glory of God in a profound experience of love.

Bernard of Clairvaux was a mystic but only within the definition of a mystic suggested by Allison Peers: "A mystic is a person who has fallen in love with God."[2] He reminds us that we are not afraid of lovers; indeed, they attract us by their single-mindedness, their ardor, and their yearning to be with the object of their love. So it was with Bernard. His single abbey in Clairvaux grew to 350 abbeys in his lifetime because of the charter of love instituted there. Like John before him, Bernard was an apostle of love. He too turned his face toward God. Truly, he exemplified love as the ultimate motivation of a life devoted to God.

DISCIPLINES OF THE SPIRIT

The Book of Acts was addressed to a lover of God, Theophilus, and in it is described the spiritual disciplines practiced by first-century Christians to nourish their love for the Lord. There were four disciplines which they practiced—Bible study, cell-group fellowship, the Lord's Supper, and prayer (Acts 2:42). Bible study is referred to as the apostles' teaching, leading Christians, like those at Berea (Acts 17:11), to examine the Scriptures every day to see if what the apostles taught was true. Bible study and prayer are the two universal disciplines for all of God's people in all cultures at all times. When the Emmaus disciples walked with Jesus in Luke 24, He explained to them what was said about Him in the Old Testament Scriptures. This is the richest devotional approach to Bible reading, to seek Jesus in every chapter. I would like to have been there when Jesus pointed Himself out in the Old Testament writings. He can be found on every page. Sometimes He is hiding, but He is there. That's the point of Norman Geisler's book *To Understand the Bible Look for Jesus.*[3]

Bible reading is best punctuated by prayer. P.T. Forsyth once declared that "prayer is to the Christian what original research is to the scientist." It gets us down to bedrock reality. And Donald Bloesch has given us one of the finest definitions of prayer: "heartfelt conversation with God as a Personal Being."[4] Whatever other religious exercises we may practice, without these two basic ones, Bible study and prayer, the others are empty and powerless.

But there are others. Koinonea—Christian cell-group fellowship—and the Eucharist—the Lord's Supper—are both found in Acts 2. Later in the eighteenth century, John Wesley included these among his five works of piety for the Holy Clubs at Oxford. His small conference groups were inspired by Zinzendorf's

community at Herrnhut, Germany. Eventually, they developed into
an organized progression from Society to Class Meeting to Band.
The smaller groupings were to make it possible for believers to
share their spiritual pilgrimage and to encourage one another in
their love for God. They were the basis of the great Wesleyan
revivals and the key to their organizational strength. In many ways,
they were a precursor of the modern church growth movement in
which single large congregations are broken down into multiple
intimate cell groups. Wesley also emphasized the Lord's Supper,
participating in it himself three or four times a week. He believed
in neither transubstantiation nor consubstantiation, but he taught
the real presence of Christ at His table. To Wesley, the soul's love
for God was rekindled in the presence of Christ and the emblems
of His sacrifice for us.

John Wesley's other three works of piety were Bible study,
prayer, and fasting. Fasting was a regular practice for him two days
a week. It was a partial fast and was intended to aid him in his quest
for Christian perfection which to him meant the perfection of his
love for God. Fast days for the body became feast days for the soul.
It was the regularized practice of these five methods for developing
a more perfect love relationship with God that led to his followers
being called Methodists.

John Wesley's disciplines emerged from his acquaintance with
both the Scriptures and the medieval Christian mystics. Among his
favorite devotional books were Thomas a Kempis' *Imitation of
Christ,* Jeremy Taylor's *Holy Living* and *Holy Dying,* and William
Law's *Serious Call to a Devout and Holy Life.* The Christian
mystics had developed a threefold classical approach to spirituality
comprising a whole range of spiritual exercises. These were summarized in the fourteenth-century classic *Theologica Germanica*,
which Martin Luther said, next to the Bible and Augustine's *Confessions,* was to him the most helpful devotional book he possessed. It
has been called the "golden book of German divinity." In it the
writer moves from the purgative stage (renewal through confrontation of sin) to the illuminative stage (the enlightening and sanctifying work of the Holy Spirit) to the unitive stage (experience of
the fullest degree of oneness with Christ).

Each stage is marked by three separate experiences. Purgation includes remorse for sin, confession of sin, and turning from sin. In all ages, confrontation with sin is the beginning of spiritual renewal. Enlightenment includes eschewing evil works, doing good works, and resisting the devil's wiles. All relate to the Holy Spirit's ministry as the One called alongside us to strengthen us.

The third stage—the unitive one—consists of singleness and purity of heart, which is centering Christ in our inner lives; love for God, in which, as in the experience of the bride in the Song of Solomon, Christ becomes chief among 10,000 to us; and contemplation, by which mystics meant an ecstatic experience of the wareness of God's presence. Contemplation is not unlike what many evangelicals today refer to as a mountaintop experience.

These stages—purgation, illumination, and union—are not chronological steps to godliness but simultaneous experiences leading to both self-renunciation and self-fulfillment. They all are part of the disciplined Christian life.

A little over a century ago the Keswick Convention for Practical Holiness was born. It became the basis of a continuous renewal of Christian life in England and the source of an unending stream of missionary volunteers. Today it draws nearly 10,000 people each summer to a little village on the shores of Lake Derwentwater, 250 miles north of London. There for five intensive days, Christians pursue a series of themes. Because the themes are meant to be provocative and lead to soul searching, I have converted them into questions. The first day is built around the question, "Is there any sin in my life that needs confession today?" The second day poses the question, "Am I taking advantage of God's provision for victory over sin?" The third day asks, "Is Jesus Christ Lord of everything in my life?" The fourth day, "Am I filled with the Holy Spirit?" and the fifth day, "Am I willing to make sacrifices in my service for Christ?" Responding to each serves as a spiritual exercise. Because Keswick is viewed as a spiritual clinic, the same questions are in order each year. Similar to a medical clinic where the attending physician takes the same tests and asks the same routine questions annually to check up on the health of his patient, Keswick has become a point of check-up and corrective surgery under the Great Physician.

In 1980 the role of spiritual disciplines was affirmed once again by Richard Foster, an evangelical Quaker. His book *Celebration of Discipline* became a bestseller and introduced a new generation of Americans to a structured life of Christian devotion. He emphasized twelve different disciplines, including most of those mentioned so far and insisted that twentieth-century believers could well be engaged in all of them.

An intriguing book of the fifteenth century was entitled *The Spiritual Exercises of St. Ignatius.* It is a stimulating thirty-day cycle of meditations based upon the life and death of Jesus. The important question, however, is not "What are St. Ignatius' spiritual exercises?" but "What are *your* spiritual exercises?" Spiritual exercises for the soul are like physical exercises for the body. What helps one person may not help another. And what helps at one stage of life may not help at a later one. Physical exercises need to be adapted individually. The same is so with spiritual exercises. We need to discover those disciplines that deepen our sense of personal relationship with God and that quicken our love for Him. Then we will be walking in the tradition of the first-century believers of Acts 2.

SOURCES OF RENEWAL
Since the close of World War II, a spiritual renewal movement has quietly gone on in America expressing itself in a host of dynamic ways. From the human viewpoint, this turn inward probably grew out of a pervasive dissatisfaction with the attainments of modern man, a disillusionment about the future of a technologically oriented society, and a rejection of material goals in favor of nonmaterial values. The youth revolt of the '60s dramatized this turn and in its wake left many adults also questioning their commitments. In our kind of troubled world, the traditional values of success, wealth, and personal fulfillment no longer satisfy. Galbraith's anatomy of power—personality, property, and organization[6]—do not seem adequate for our world changing responsibilities.

As a result many have turned to inner sources of spiritual power. While some have moved in non-Christian directions, the Holy Spirit has used this spiritual restiveness to bring people into a more authentic and vital relationship with Himself. This has been evidenced not only in the powerful charismatic movement, with its quest for the discovery and use of the gifts of the Spirit, but in such diverse movements as the rise of small groups with their stress on koinonia and Christian fellowship; the Bible fellowship programs that have brought together outside of our church Bible schools nearly 30 million people for regular study of the Word of God; the eldership concept with its focus upon a vital and accountable church structure; the discipleship movement, with its individualized programs of Christian growth; the many forms of a simple lifestyle developed so that more money could be given to the needy; the rising social conscience among evangelicals that has opened the doors to compassionate and loving ministry to hurting people; the new political expressions of concern about social crises that have become moral issues—nuclear warfare, abortion, genetic engineering, environmental destruction, poverty, racism, and world relief; and the centers of spiritual renewal that have sprung up all over the world to call Christians into a daily living walk with the Saviour. Oswald Hoffman once said in connection with a study of Acts 2, "Wherever the Holy Spirit is, the possibility exists for something new to happen." And the Holy Spirit is at work today all over the world in diverse, powerful, and dynamic spiritual movements that are leading people to commit their lives wholeheartedly to Christ and to the values of His kingdom.

As a result, in addition to renewal movements taking place in almost every major denomination, new resources for spiritual renewal are available to God's people. These also take many forms:

1. *Spiritual formation in seminaries.* One of the bright signs on the horizon of preparing pastors for ministry to their congregations is a new emphasis in theological schools on the inner spiritual life of their students. Among evangelical schools, this takes the form of a three-year curriculum in one seminary where students are guided in personal spiritual growth during their entire program, in another by a fully developed and staffed Department of Prayer and Spiritual Life, and in another by the establishment of an endowed Professorship of Prayer. Two dozen other seminaries are in the process of developing specific programs of Christian spirituality. There is a growing consensus that in the preparation of Christian workers for the world's harvest fields the emphasis of theological schools must

be upon *both* the life of the mind *and* the life of the heart. The subtitle of Kenneth Pike's book *With Heart and Mind* is "A Personal Synthesis of Scholarship and Devotion."[7] It suggests a dynamic redirection from the past in which what was every teacher's business—the spiritual development of their students—became no one's business.

Three different studies over a twenty-year period by the Association of Theological Schools revealed that, while seminaries generally were academic communities, they were not spiritual communities. This tragic disfunction has been caused by such factors as patterning the seminary after the university graduate school model, the explosion of knowledge that forced older devotional classes out of the curriculum to make way for new emphases, the narrowing of a teacher's concern for holistic education due to his or her intense specialization, a prevailing negative reaction to pietism in academic circles, and reward systems that penalize student-oriented teachers in favor of research-oriented ones. Seminarians often emerged from these programs with sharpened understandings of God, His Word, and His world but not necessarily as people of a deep inner life of personal devotion to the Lord.

All of that is changing. In a recent review of thirty-one seminary catalogs, I counted sixty-nine different courses in the field of spiritual development cumulatively available to students. They clustered around four basic areas: spiritual formation, prayer, the history of spirituality, and its application to ministry. In many ways, the emergence of such courses is the result of student concern and hunger. They have been most aware of their barrenness of soul. Engaged in heavy academic programs, often having family responsibilities, working sometimes full time at night to earn funds and frequently commuting long distances to school, students have found it difficult to maintain the kind of rich devotional life that centers everything upon Christ and upon love for Him. Hence, the new direction will unite the heart and its love with the mind and its understanding in the seminary program.

That means a new generation of ministers will have more to offer the people who themselves are hungering for a more satisfying personal life with Christ and a deeper love for Him. Pastors will be as concerned about the inner spiritual integrity of their people as

they are about their witness, service, stewardship, or social awareness. And they will have more to offer out of their own revitalized
pilgrimage with God.

2. *Spiritual direction.* An additional resource closely related to
the first is the new emphasis upon spiritual direction gaining
momentum in Protestant and evangelical churches. It is different
from the traditional concept of discipling with its introduction to a
wide variety of Christian concerns. Spiritual direction consists of a
one-on-one relationship with exclusive attention upon the soul's
growth. The spiritual director is a catalyst who through listening,
discussing, and praying helps the seeking Christian to evaluate his
inner progress with God and to seek new cutting edges of spiritual
growth. Ideally, it is a three-way partnership—the director, the
directee, and the Holy Spirit. In its highest contemporary forms,
spiritual direction is not autocratic and authoritarian but humble,
flexible, and responsive to the Spirit. The director may be a pastor,
a trained professional, or a dedicated layperson. Some Protestant
churches are now employing staff persons to give full-time spiritual
direction within the congregation. Others provide part-time directors. The new partnership brings accountability more directly into
the Christian life and assists the directee to keep his focus upon
love for God.

3. *Spritual retreat centers.* There are now available to
laypersons and Christian workers spiritual retreat centers scattered
all over the world, perhaps as many as 1,500 in the United States
alone. They provide periods of withdrawal from normal activities
to engage in devotional exercises for the cultivation of a love
relationship with God.

Biblical precursors of the modern retreat movement can be
found in the periods of solitude observed by Moses, Elijah, John the
Baptist, the Apostle Paul, and Jesus Christ Himself. In the early
years of the Christian church, spiritual solitude was nourished by
the desert fathers and by monastic communities. Retreats became a
renewing force within Roman Catholicism during the Counter-
Reformation and were systematized under the influence of St.
Ignatius Loyola and his Spiritual Exercises. In the midnineteenth-
century, retreats appeared in the Church of England. To this day,
the formal retreat movement of the West is centered largely in

these two churches. Increasingly, however, other churches and parachurch groups are adopting variant forms of the classical retreat to encourage the spiritual growth of their members.

Thus, a movement once limited to persons whose primary vocation was Christian ministry, today involves devout lay persons in all walks of life, including an increasing number of them with the evangelical movement.

The primary focus of a retreat upon the enrichment of one's devotion to God has been blurred in contemporary church practice by the indiscriminate use of this term for many different kinds of group experiences. Currently, the word *retreat* is used to describe such diverse activities as recreational outings, intensive Bible studies, encounter groupings, behavioral laboratories, marriage enrichment sessions, dream therapy planning workshops, and hide-away housing. But these experiences—good as they may be— do not constitute retreats in the classical sense.

The Church of the Savior in Washington, D.C. has been noted for its more classical retreats. It operates two centers outside the city—Dayspring, founded more than twenty-five years ago and Wellspring, begun more recently. One of the requirements of church membership is to spend a period of quiet spiritual reflection at one of these centers. In the Twin Cities of Minnesota, the Hennepin Avenue Methodist Church operates such a center fifty miles out of the city with a pastor assigned full-time to its direction. The Mount Olivet Lutheran Church has invested nearly $2,000,000 in a similar retreat center twenty-five miles south of the church. Both churches use their centers exclusively for spiritual life retreats.

Two private colleges—both Quaker in origin—are identified with retreat centers. The Yokefellow Center is on the campus of Earlham College in Indiana and Tillicum is but a few miles from George Fox College in Oregon. Both are dedicated primarily to the nourishment of the inner life.

Retreats may be private or corporate, unstructured or guided, observed in silence or shared in conversation, inclusive of manual labor or concentrated upon spiritual disciplines. The ultimate purpose of the retreat is to deepen one's love relationship with God. In so doing, it channels spiritual power into the life of the retreatant, enabling him to affirm his love for God and to deny his love for the world.

Most of these centers are filled when retreats are offered, and some have to waitlist registrants desiring to get in. They supplement the ministry of the parish church by providing a more leisurely time for spiritual reflection than the normal Sunday program allows. Only in recent years have retreat directors begun to meet on an ecumenical basis. Occasionally, a complete directory of retreat centers in the United States is published.[8]

4. *The devotional classic.* Another source of fuel to feed the flame of devotion is to be found in the classics of Christian devotion that span twenty centuries of church history. Happily, the Western church is beginning to read again the devotional writings of the Christian mystics and to learn from their experiences about the riches of life in Christ. Religious bookstores are devoting more shelf space to these books on the inner life in response to the heart hunger of God's people.

I am delighted that the greatest classics are being made available again to contemporary Christians as a result of some major publishing ventures. These include ones still in process, the sixty-volume set being released by Paulist Press, *Classics of Western Spirituality.*[9] These are faithful translations of the greatest devotional classics in Christian history, together with a few representative non-Christian writings about spirituality. Each volume contains a full introduction to the author and his times. Similarly, Multnomah Press has begun to publish a series of twenty proposed volumes, *Classics of Faith and Devotion.*[10] These are edited and updated by James Houston, chancellor of Regents College, and are accompanied by a personal witness to their value by some Christian leader in America. Broadman Press has completed its twelve-volume series, *Christian Classics,*[11] in which it brought together 200 texts under major categories, such as "Pietism" and "English Puritan Tradition." Also completed is the *Doubleday Devotional Classics* series[12] edited by E. Glenn Hinson, devoted to ten major devotional writings from Richard Baxter in the seventeenth century to Thomas Kelly in the twentieth. This republication of devotional classics, together with individual volumes updated by such authors as Sherwood Wirt and Donald Demaray, means a new accessibility to the rich spiritual treasures of the past.

We must read devotional classics differently than we read other books. Our entire personalities must be involved with the authors. Like works of art, their books must act upon us. A devotional approach to reading the classics—like savoring our food—requires reading slowly, affectionately, concentratedly, repeatedly, attentively, expectantly, and humbly. A helpful prayer to precede devotional reading—much like grace before a meal—was suggested by Charles Whiston, himself a modern mystic:

> *O God, grant that I may sit*
> *humbly at the feet of Thy servant (Fenelon)*
> *and be taught by him of Thee,*
> *his Lord and mine. Amen.*[13]

As we see what the writing saints saw, we discover that through the centuries Christians have placed a continuous and unbroken emphasis upon self-control. This rich, mystical tradition can make a vital contribution to meeting our present-day need for self-discipline both in our nation and in our churches. The voices of the past encourage us to say *yes* to our Lord and *no* to ourselves.

Thus, there are valuable resources for the earnest Christian who out of a deeply motivating love for Christ desires to live a life of voluntary self-discipline in our world. These consist of appropriate disciplines of the spirit and varied sources of renewal available to everyone. As we draw upon them, we begin to live simultaneously in two worlds—one subject to our five physical senses and one open to our sixth intuitive sense of faith. Our lives then are ordered not by the shifting values of our world but by the eternal values of Christ's kingdom. It is then that we are most able to say *no* to our culture.

FOR FURTHER READING

Daniel Baumann, *Clearing Life's Hurdles* (Ventura, CA: Regal Books, 1984), 165 pages.

D.G. Kehl, *Control Yourself* (Grand Rapids, MI: Zondervan Publishing House, 1982), 233 pages.

Bernard L. Ramm, *The Right, the Good, the Happy* (Waco, Tex.: Word Publishing, 1971), 165 pages.

NOTES

Chapter One ☐

1. Charles Swindoll, *The Seasons of Life* (Portland: Multnomah Press, 1983), 94.
2. David Reisman, quoted in "A Red Light for Scofflaws," *Time,* Jan. 24, 1983, 94.
3. Lawrence J. Hatterer, M.D., *The Pleasurable Addicts* (New York: A.S. Barnes and Co., 1980), 17.
4. Carl F.H. Henry, "The Crisis of Modern Learning" in *Imprints,* Hillsdale College, Hillsdale, Mich., Feb. 1984, 1.
5. Bruce Hafner, "The Family, Private Education and Public Schools," in *Vital Speeches of the Day* (Long Island, N.Y.: City News Publishing Co.), Dec. 15, 1983, 152.
6. Mark Cameron, "Crime and the Decline of Values," in *Vital Speeches of the Day,* August 15, 1981, 651.
7. William Bennett, "To Reclaim a Legacy" *The Chronicle of Higher Education,* Nov. 28, 1984, 16.
8. John Taylor and Richard Usher, "Discipline," *Encyclopedia of Educational Research* (New York: Free Press, 1982), vol. 5, 45.
9. John Naisbitt, *Megatrends* (New York: Warner Books, 1982), 234.
10. Sean O'Sullivan, "Crime and the Decline of Values," quoted in Mark Cameron, *Vital Speeches*

of the Day, Aug. 15, 1981, 651.

11. Grace and Fred Hechinger, *Teenage Tyranny* (New York: William Morrow and Co., 1963), 210.

12. Roger Rosenblatt, "The Most Amazing Sixty Years in History," *Time*, Oct. 1983, 26-27.

13. Armand M. Nicholi, quoted by Carl Henry in *Quest for Reality* (Downers Grove, Ill: InterVarsity Press, 1973), 7.

14. Francis Schaeffer, *The Great Evangelical Disaster* (Westchester, Ill.: Crossway Books, 1984), 21.

15. Elizabeth Elliot, *Discipline, the Glad Surrender* (Old Tappan, N.J.: Fleming H. Revell Co., 1982), 24.

16. Richard Shelley Taylor, *The Disciplined Life* (Kansas City: Beacon Hill Press, 1962), 26-27.

17. David Watson, *Discipleship* (London: Hodder and Stoughton, 1981), 15.

Chapter Two ☐ 1. Peter Lawford, quoted in "Peter Lawford Graduates from Drug Abuse Center," *St. Paul Dispatch*, Jan. 23, 1984, 10a.

2. Ansley Cuddingham Moore, "The Case Against Drinking," *Christian Century*, Nov. 19, 1952, 1349.

3. Cynthia Parsons, "College—Where Drinking Is (Not) Part of the Social Life," *Christian Science Monitor*, Nov. 3, 1980, 16.

4. Betty Ford, *The Times of My Life* (New York: Harper & Row Publishing Co., 1978), 287.

5. Viveca Ekers, "Eat, Drink, and Be Wary," *Environmental Action*, June 1982, 3.

6. "Liquor Trade Out of Control," *Miami Herald*, Oct. 19, 1980, 16a.

7. "Alcoholism—Counting the Cost," *The Rotarian*, Sept. 1984, 16.

8. Asa Bushnell, "Back from Skid Row," *The Rotarian*, Sept. 1980, 14.

Chapter Three ☐ 1. *Time*, March 19, 1984, 26.

2. Joel Brinkler, "The War on Narcotics: Can It Be Won?" *New York Times*, Sept. 1984, 12.

3. "War on the Cocaine Mafia," *Time*, May 28,

1984, 62.

4. "US: Cuba Still Fosters Drug Trade," *Miami Herald*, Feb. 22, 1984, 1.

5. Hardin B. and Helen Jones, *Sensual Drugs* (Cambridge: Cambridge University Press, 1977), 2.

6. Melvin H. Weinswig, *Use and Misuse of Drugs Subject to Abuse* (New York: Pegasus, 1973), 7.

7. Robert Du Pont, "Sounding the Alarm: Marijuana Is Far from Harmless," *Social Issues Resource Series, PTA Today*, May 1981, 3.

8. Gabriel Nahas, "Some Specific Reasons to Keep off the 'Grass,'" *Social Issues Resource Series*, vol. 3, 5.

9. Du Pont, *Social Issues Resource Series*, 3.

10. Don Reese, quoted by Marc Lepson in "Cocaine: Drug of the '80s" Editorial Research Project vol. II-8, *Social Issues Resource Series*, Aug. 27, 1982, 639.

11. Eileen Orgintz, "Cocaine's Appeal Sifts into the Mainstream," *Miami Herald*, May 5, 1981, C3.

12. Charles Schuster, quoted in "Cocaine's Appeal Sifts into the Mainstream," *Miami Herald*, May 5, 1981, C3.

13. Rita Rooney, "Women and Cocaine," *Ladies Home Journal*, March 1984, 119.

14. Pete Axthelm, "Cocaine and Basketball," *Newsweek*, Sept. 1, 1980, 77.

15. "A Story That Shocked the Nation's Capital," *U.S. News and World Report*, Oct. 13, 1980, 56.

16. McLean and Bower, *High on the Campus* (Wheaton, Ill.: Tyndale, 1970), 4-7.

Chapter Four □

1. "Ask McGee about MLT," *Sun Country Magazine*, Nov.-Dec. 1984, 8.

2. Peter Axthelm, "An American in Trouble" *Newsweek*, April 25, 1983, 81.

3. *U.S. News and World Report*, May 30, 1983, 27.

4. Jon Halliday and Peter Fuller, *The Psychology of Gambling* (London: Penguin, 1974), 12.

5. James Mann and Gordon Bock, "The Gambling Rage," *U.S. News and World Report*, May 30, 1983, 31.

6. Scott Morris and Nicolas Charney, "Stop It!

Swearing off Gambling," *Psychology Today,* May 1983, 88.

7. James Mann and Gordon Beck, op. cit., 30.
8. Jon Halliday and Peter Fuller, op. cit., 12.
9. *U.S. News and World Report,* Aug. 15, 1980, 40.
10. John Greene, "The Gambling Trap," *Psychology Today,* Sept. 1982, 50.
11. John Greene, op. cit., 51.
12. John Winters, "Beating the System," *Journal of Current Social Issues,* Summer 1979, 17.
13. "A Corrupt System" editorial in the *Baptist Messenger,* Nov. 22, 1984, 2.
14. James Mann and Gordon Bock, op. cit., 29.
15. "Gambling Industry Bets Public Will Okay Expansion," *Eternity,* April 1984, 13.
16. Larry Bradfast quoted in "Churches Gear up to Combat a Push by Gambling Interests," *Christianity Today,* Feb. 17, 1984, 46.
17. Cardinal Cushing, quoted by Starkey, Lycuraus, *Money, Mania and Morals* (N.Y.: Abingdon, 1964) 92.
18. Arthur Holmes, "Why Oppose Gambling?" *Eternity,* June 1977, 27.
19. Methodist Declaration, quoted in E. Benson Perkins, *Gambling in English Life* (London: Epworth Press, 1958), 100.
20. Edith Schaeffer, *Lifelines* (Westchester, Ill.: Crossway Books, 1982), 197.
21. J. Clark Gibson, "Gambling and Citizenship," a Becky pamphlet (London: Epworth Press, 1956), 10.

Chapter Five □

1. Patti Roberts, *Ashes to Gold* (Waco, Tex.: Word, 1983), 119.
2. Malcolm Muggeridge, *Something Beautiful for God* (London: Collins, 1975), 74-75.
3. Kenneth Galbraith, *The Anatomy of Power* (Boston: Houghton Mifflin Co., 1983), 206.
4. Stephen Neill, *Christian Holiness* (New York: Harper & Row, 1960), 127.
5. Barbara Ward, *The Rich Nations and the Poor Nations* (New York: W.W. Norton & Co., 1967), 23.

Chapter Six ☐

1. Ron Enroth, "All Isn't Well in a Popular Christian Diet Program," *Christianity Today*. April 9, 1982.

2. Donald B. Ardell, *High Level Wellness* (Emmaus, Pa.: Rodale Press, 1977), 5.

3. Don Ethan Miller, *Body Mind* (Englewood Cliffs, N.J.: Prentice Hall, 1974), 199.

4. John J. Pilch, *Wellness: An Introduction to a Full Life* (Minneapolis: Winston Press, 1981), 17.

5. Judith Rudin, quoted in Benjamin Walman, *Psychological Aspects of Obesity* (New York: Van Nostrand Reinhold Co., 1982), 30.

6. Albert J. Stunkard, quoted in Richard Stuart, *Slim Chance in a Fat World* (Champaign, Ill.: Research Press, 1972), 240.

7. Charlie Shedd, *The Fat Is in Your Head* (Waco, Tex.: Word Publishing, 1978), 142.

8. *Francis de Sales* (Chicago: Regnery Co., 1957), 33.

9. Stephen Neill, *Christian Holiness* (New York: Harper Brothers, 1960), 126.

10. Steve Harper, *Devotional Life in the Wesleyan Tradition* (Nashville: Upper Room, 1983), 50.

11. Richard Foster, *Celebration of Discipline* (New York: Harper & Row, 1978), 48.

12. Arthur Wallis, *God's Chosen Fast* (Fort Washington, Pa.: Christian Literature Crusade, 1974), 84-92.

13. McClintock and Strong, *Cycolpaedia of Biblical Theology & Ecclesiastical Literature* (New York: Harper & Row Publishers, 1981), *John Calvin* (vol. III), 492.

14. Walter Stanley Mooneyham, *What Do You Say to a Hungry World?* (Waco, Tex.: Word, 1975).

Chapter Seven ☐

1. Richard Anderson, Letter to the Editor, *Equal Time News*. Jan. 11, 1984, Issue 46, 4.

2. William Baird, *The Corinthian Church—a Biblical Approach to Urban Culture* (New York: Abingdon Press, 1964).

3. William Herberg, "Recipe for Disaster," *Christianity Today* May 7, 1971, 25.

4. Edith Schaeffer, op. cit.

5. Justin Smith, "The Playboy Legacy," *St. Paul Pioneer Press*, May 1, 1983, 4d.

6. Hugh Hefner, quoted in William S. Banowski, *It's a Playboy World* (Old Tappan, N.J.: Fleming H. Revell Co., 1973), 114.

7. *USA Today*, October 19, 1984, D2.

8. Banowski, op. cit., 83.

9. *Christianity Today*, October 5, 1984, 17.

10. "Why Married Men Will Still Pay for Sex," *Ladies Home Journal*, March 1984, 62-63.

11. Esther Wattenberg, "Ordinance Mixes Up the Characters in Porn Debate," *Minneapolis Star and Tribune*, Jan. 11, 1984, 19a.

12. "Citizens Concerned for Community Values" July 1984, 6, A paper presented at second National Consultation on Obscenity, Pornography, and Indecency, Cincinnati, Sept. 6, 1984.

13. Ibid., 6.

14. "Rape and Men's Magazine Readership," *Arizona Republic*, Dec. 9, 1983.

15. "Citizens Concerned for Community Values," op. cit., 13.

16. Mitchell Ditkoff, "Child Pornography," *American Humane*, Apr. 1978, 80.

17. Alfred Kinsey, quoted in Sani Weisenberg, "Growing Up Gay," *Miami Herald*, Oct. 16, 1983.

18. Louis Smedes, *Sex for Christians* (Grand Rapids: William B. Eerdmans Publishing Co., 1980), 42.

19. Irving Bieber, *Homosexuality: A Psychoanalytic Study of Male Homosexuals* (New York: Vintage Books, 1965), 319.

20. Barbara Somerville, "Kinsey Gives Report on Homosexuals," *West Palm Beach Post*, Feb. 16, 1982, b5.

21. "Incest: Out of Hiding," *Science News*, April 5, 1980, 218.

22. Richard Phillips, "Incest," *Chicago Tribune*, Sept. 20, 1981.

23. Linda Kohl, "The Incest Cycle," *St. Paul Dispatch*, Feb. 1, 1984, 6a.

24. Charles Whiston, *Prayer: A Study of Distinctive Christian Prayer* (Grand Rapids: William B. Eerdmans Publishing Co., 1972), 123.

25. Ibid.

Chapter Eight ☐
1. Linda Mercadante, *From Hierarchy to Equality* (Vancouver: G-M-H Books, 1980), 160.
2. *Better Homes and Gardens,* July-August 1983.
3. John Naisbitt, *Megatrends: Ten New Directions Transforming Our Lives* (New York: Warner Books, 1982), 223.
4. Dietrich Bonhoeffer, *Letters and Papers from Prison* (London: Fontana, 1964), 150.
5. Zane Alexander, *Till Death Do Us Part or Something Else Comes Up* (Philadelphia: Westminster Press, 1976).
6. Mansell Pattison, quoted in Tom Minnery, "Homosexuals Can Change," *Christianity Today,* Feb. 6, 1981, 38.

Chapter Nine ☐
1. Stephen Neill, op. cit., 117.
2. George B. Cutten, *Instincts and Religion* (New York: Harper & Row Publishers, 1940), 26.
3. L.E. Maxwell, *Born Crucified* (Chicago: Moody Press, 1945), 85-86.
4. Neill, 133.
5. Ruth Paxton, *Life on the Highest Plane*, Chicago: Bible Institute Colportage Association, 1941), 166.
6. Kepler, Thomas, *The Fellowship of the Saints* (New York: Abingdon-Cokesbury, 1948), 7.

Chapter Ten ☐
1. Gordon Wakefield, *The Westminister Dictionary of Spirituality* (Philadelphia: Westminster Press, 1983), 220.
2. Augustine, translated by Sherwood Wirt, *Love Song* (New York: Harper & Row Publishers, 1971), 116.
3. Benedict of Nusia, quoted in Thomas S. Kepler, *Fellowship of the Saints* (New York: Abingdon Press, 1948), 102.
4. Donald E. Demaray, paraphrase of *The Imitation of Christ* by Thomas a Kempis (Grand Rapids: Baker Book House, 1982), 240.
5. Lawrence Scupoli, *The Spiritual Combat* (New York: Paulist Press, 1978), 6.
6. Ibid.

7. Richard Baxter, *The Reformed Pastor,* edited by James M. Houston, (Portland. Ore.: Multnomah Press, 1982), 35-36.

8. William Law, *A Serious Call to a Devout and Holy Life* (Philadelphia: Westminster Press, 1948), 30-31.

9. Emily Herman, *Creative Prayer* (Cincinnati: Forward Movement Publications), 93.

10. Evan Hopkins, *The Law of Liberty in the Spiritual Life* (Philadelphia: *S.S. Times*, 1952), 56.

11. A.W. Tozer, *Of God and Men* (Harrisburg: Christian Publications 1960), 39.

12. Wakefield, op. cit., 382.

Chapter Eleven ☐ 1. Bernard of Clairvaux, *The Love of God* (Portland, Ore.: Multnomah Press, 1983), 154-159.

2. Allison Peers, *Spirit of Flame* (Wilton, Conn: Morehouse-Barlow, Inc., 1946), 150.

3. Norman Geisler, *To Understand the Bible Look for Jesus* (Downers Grove, Ill.: InterVarsity Press).

4. Donald Bloesch, *Crisis of Piety* (Grand Rapids: Eerdmans, 1968), 69.

5. Anonymous, *Theologica Germanica* (Cleveland: World Publishing Co., 1952), 31.

6. John Galbraith, *The Anatomy of Power* (Boston: Houghton Mifflin, Co., 1983), xi.

7. Kenneth Pike, *With Heart and Mind* (Grand Rapids: Eerdmans, 1962).

8. Philip Deemer, *Ecumenical Directory of Retreat and Conference Centers* (San Francisco: Jarrow Press, 1984), 257.

9. *Classics of Western Spirituality* (New York, Paulist Press).

10. *Classics of Faith and Devotion* (Portland, Ore.: Multnomah Press).

11. *Christian Classics* (Nashville: Broadman).

12. *Doubleday Devotional Classics* (Garden City, NY: Doubleday and Co.).

13. Charles Whiston, *Pray* (Grand Rapids: Eerdmans, 1972), 108.